This Is Real and You Are Completely Unprepared

THIS IS REAL AND YOU ARE COMPLETELY UNPREPARED

THE DAYS OF AWE AS A JOURNEY OF TRANSFORMATION

ALAN LEW

LITTLE, BROWN AND COMPANY

BOSTON • NEW YORK • LONDON

FIRST EDITION

COPYRIGHT ACKNOWLEDGMENTS ARE ON PAGE 277.

Library of Congress Cataloging-in-Publication Data
Lew, Alan.
    This is real and you are completely unprepared : the Days of Awe as a
journey of transformation / by Alan Lew.
        p.   cm.
    ISBN 0-316-73908-1
    1. High Holidays. 2. Spiritual life — Judaism. 3. Repentance — Judaism.
I. Title.
BM693.H5L49 2003
296.4'31 — dc21   2003040028

Q-FF

TEXT DESIGN BY MERYL SUSSMAN LEVAVI/DIGITEXT

PRINTED IN THE UNITED STATES OF AMERICA

For Sherril

My life and my breath

Contents

This Is Real and You Are Completely Unprepared

CHAPTER ONE

THE SOUL
STRETCHES OUT
TO CONTAIN ITSELF

A MAP OF THE JOURNEY

YOU ARE WALKING THROUGH THE WORLD HALF ASLEEP. It isn't just that you don't know who you are and that you don't know how or why you got here. It's worse than that; these questions never even arise. It is as if you are in a dream.

Then the walls of the great house that surrounds you crumble and fall. You tumble out onto a strange street, suddenly conscious of your estrangement and your homelessness.

A great horn sounds, calling you to remembrance, but all you can remember is how much you have forgotten. Every day for a month, you sit and try to remember who you are and where you are going. By the last week of this month, your need to know these things weighs upon you. Your prayers become urgent.

Then the great horn sounds in earnest one hundred times. The time of transformation is upon you. The world is once again cracking through the shell of its egg to be born. The gate between heaven and earth creaks open. The Book of Life and the Book of Death are opened once again, and your name is written in one of them.

But you don't know which one.

The ten days that follow are fraught with meaning and dread. They are days when it is perfectly clear every second that you live in the midst of a chain of ineluctable consequence, that everything you do, every prayer you utter, every intention you form, every act of compassion you perform, ripples out from the center of your being to the end of time. Anger and its terrible cost lie naked before you. Grievance gives way to forgiveness. At the same time, you become aware that you also stand at the end of a long chain of consequences. Many things are beyond your control. They are part of a process that was set in motion long ago. You find the idea of this unbearable.

Then, just when you think you can't tolerate this one moment more, you are called to gather with a multitude in a great hall. A court has convened high up on the altar in the front of the hall. Make way! Make way! the judges of the court proclaim, for everyone must be included in the proceeding. No one, not even the usual outcasts, may be excluded. You are told that you are in possession of a great power, the power of speech, and that you will certainly abuse it — you are already forgiven for having abused it in the past — but in the end it will save you.

For the next twenty-four hours you rehearse your own death. You wear a shroud and, like a dead person, you neither eat nor drink nor fornicate. You summon the desperate strength of life's last moments. A great wall of speech is hurled against your heart again and again; a fist beats against the wall of your heart relentlessly until you are broken-hearted and confess to your great crime. You are a human being, guilty of every crime imaginable. Your heart is cracking through its shell to be reborn. Then a chill grips you. The gate between heaven and earth has suddenly begun to close. The multitude has swollen. It is almost as if the great hall has magically expanded to include an infinity of desperate souls. This is your last chance. Everyone has run out of time. Every heart has broken. The gate clangs shut, the great horn sounds one last time. You feel curiously lighthearted and clean.

Some days later you find yourself building a house; a curious house, an incomplete house, a house that suggests the idea of a house without actually being one. This house has no roof. There are a few twigs and branches on top, but you can see the stars and feel the wind through them. And the walls of this house don't go all the way around it either. Yet as you sit in this house eating the bounty of the earth, you feel a deep sense of security and joy. Here in this mere idea of a house, you finally feel as if you are home. The journey is over.

At precisely this moment, the journey begins again. The curious house is dismantled. The King calls you in for a last intimate meal, and then you set out on your way again.

This may all sound like a dream — a nightmare — and it is. It is a deep dream of human existence. It is also a description of the round of Jewish rituals that are observed every year between mid-summer and midfall — roughly early August to mid-October, although this varies slightly from year to year. It is a gesture-by-gesture description of the stages of the Days of Awe, each one constituting a passage in this ancient journey of transformation:

5

- Tisha B'Av, the day of mourning for the destruction of the Temple in Jerusalem, the day of the crumbling of the great walls.
- Elul, the last month of the year, when the great horn of remembrance is sounded to begin the month of introspection that precedes the Days of Awe.
- Selichot, the last week of fervent prayer that precedes Rosh Hashanah.
- Rosh Hashanah itself, the head of the year, the day of remembrance; the day of the one hundred blasts and the two books.
- The Ten Days of Teshuvah, the Days of Awe proper; the period of intense spiritual transformation that begins with Rosh Hashanah and ends with Yom Kippur, ten days fraught with meaning and dread.
- Kol Nidre, the eve of Yom Kippur, when the great court is convened above and below.
- Yom Kippur itself, the Day of Atonement, the day we rehearse our own death, the day that comes to a close with the clanging shut of the great gates.
- And finally Sukkot, a joyous coda to the journey, the autumnal harvest festival, during which we build and inhabit the sukkah, a booth, the barest outline of a house.

❧

R. Buckminster Fuller's students once asked him to name the most important figure of the twentieth century. Sigmund Freud, he said without a moment's hesitation. They were shocked. Why Freud? Why not Einstein, about whom Fuller had written extensively, or

6

some other figure from the world of science or economics or architecture, to which he had devoted his considerable energy? So Fuller explained himself. Sigmund Freud, he said, was the one who had introduced the single great idea upon which all the significant developments of the twentieth century had rested: the invisible is more important than the visible. You would never have had Einstein if Freud hadn't convinced the world of this first. You would never have had nuclear physics.

For all Freud's animus against Judaism, his idea was an extremely Jewish one. In fact it may not be too much to suggest that it is *the* Jewish idea. Judaism came into the world to bring the news that the invisible is more important than the visible. From the beginning of time, humans had seen the world as a play of competing forces, which they had personified as gods. The sea struggled against the earth, the rain either overwhelmed the forests and fields or famished them, men and beasts hunted each other, hatred and vengeance, love and compassion, struggled for hegemony in the human heart. But Judaism came to say that beneath this appearance of conflict, multiplicity, and caprice there was a oneness, a singularity, all-powerful and endlessly compassionate, endlessly just.

In the visible world, we live out our routine and sometimes messy lives. We have jobs, families, and houses. Our lives seem quite ordinary and undramatic. It is only beneath the surface of this world that the real and unseen drama of our lives is unfolding, only there that the walls of the house crumble and fall, that the horn sounds one hundred times, that the gate between heaven and earth opens and the great books of life and death open as well. It is there that the court is convened, that we rehearse our own death, that the gate closes again, and that we finally come home to the mere idea of the very house that crumbled and fell in the first place. If the purpose of ritual is to render the invisible visible, then what is the profound, universal, unseen, and unspoken reality that all of this ritual reflects? What journey of the soul, what invisible journey of transformation, does all of this make visible?

On this journey our soul will awaken to itself. We will venture from innocence to sin and back to innocence again. This is a journey from denial to awareness, from self-deception to judgment. We will learn our Divine Name. We will move from self-hatred to self-forgiveness, from anger to healing, from hard-heartedness to brokenheartedness. This is the journey the soul takes to transform itself and to evolve, the journey from boredom and staleness — from deadness — to renewal. It is on the course of this journey that we confront our shadow and come to embrace it, that we come to know our deepest desires and catch a glimpse of where they come from, that we express the paradoxical miracle of our own being and the infinite power of simply being present, simply being who we are. It is the journey from little mind to big mind, from confinement in the ego to a sense of ourselves as a part of something larger. It is the journey from isolation to a sense of our intimate connection to all being. This is the journey on which we discover ourselves to be part of an inevitable chain of circumstances, the journey beyond death, the journey home. This is the longest journey we will ever make, and we must complete it in that brief instant before the gates of heaven clang shut.

The journey I will describe in these pages is one of self-discovery, spiritual discipline, self-forgiveness, and spiritual evolution. It is the snapshot the Jewish people pull out every autumn of the great journey all human beings must make across this world: the journey from Tisha B'Av to Sukkot, from Rosh Hashanah to Yom Kippur, from birth to death and back to renewal again. Seeing yourself in this snapshot will help you chart the course of your own spiritual evolution. Every soul needs to express itself. Every heart needs to crack itself open. Every one of us needs to move from anger to healing, from denial to consciousness, from boredom to renewal. These needs did not arise yesterday. They are among the most ancient of human yearnings, and they are fully expressed in the pageantry and ritual of the Days of Awe, in the great journey we make between Rosh Hashanah and Yom Kippur.

⅍

In ancient Israel the seventh month of the year was an anxious time. All the other civilizations of the ancient Near East were sustained by great rivers. The Egyptians had the Nile, the Babylonians had the Tigris and the Euphrates; but Israel was completely dependent on rain. The rains came in the eighth month. So the seventh month was a time when the nation of Israel felt its life hanging in the balance. This utter dependence on the heavens seems to have given the ancient Israelites an intense sense of their dependence on God. It may very well have been this dependence that sensitized the Israelites to the existence of God in the first place. The ancient Israelites felt themselves to be part of a vast interpenetrating whole, a cosmos in which the weather and their own moral condition were active and interdependent constituents. The round of holidays we now call the Days of Awe gave form to this sense.

Rosh Hashanah is never mentioned in the Torah. Rosh Hashanah means "the head of the year," and it marks the start of the New Year in today's Jewish calendar. But in biblical times, the New Year began exactly six months before, in Nisan, the month in which Passover occurs. The Day of Atonement — Yom Kippur — *is* mentioned in the Torah. It appears along with Passover, Shavuot, Sukkot, the New Moon, and the Sabbath in the recitations of the sacred calendar which appear in the Books of Leviticus, Numbers, and Deuteronomy.

> And the Lord spoke to Moses saying also on the tenth day of this the seventh month, there will be a day of atonement. It will be a holy gathering to you and you will afflict your souls and offer an offering made by fire to the Lord. And you will do no work on that very same day, for it is a day of atonement, to make atonement for you before the Lord your God.

While there is no mention of Rosh Hashanah in these calendars, there is a special day mentioned ten days before Yom Kippur, on the first day of the seventh month, precisely the day that would later become Rosh Hashanah. In biblical times, however, this day was called Yom Ha-Zikaron, the Day of Remembrance, or Yom Zikaron Truah, the Day of the Blowing of the Horn for Remembrance. But who was to remember what? Was it a day when God was supposed to remember us? Were we supposed to remember God? Or was it a day when we were to begin to become mindful of our moral circumstances in preparation for the Day of Atonement that would soon be upon us? Was the sound of the ram's horn (the shofar) a mystical nexus between heaven and earth or, as suggested by the Rambam (Maimonides, a medieval philosopher and legal authority and a towering figure in the world

of Jewish thought), was it a wake-up call for us? Was it crying out
to us, "Awake, awake, you sleepers from your sleep; examine your
deeds, return in repentance, remember your Creator; those of you
who forget the truth and go astray the whole year in vanity and
emptiness that neither profits nor saves, look to your souls"?

Examining the length and breadth of the tradition that
would follow — following the tradition through its biblical, talmudic, medieval, and modern periods — the answer is, clearly, all
of the above. God's mindfulness of us is the sine qua non of this
holiday season. If there were no consciousness out there aware of
us, responding to us, this whole round of holidays would make
no sense at all. Neither would life. The rains would fall at random,
the heavens would shut themselves up, and we would live and die
without meaning. Equally important is our awareness of God. We
shouldn't imagine that this was any less problematic for the ancient
Israelites than it is for us. If they found it easy, they wouldn't have
needed one hundred blasts of the great shofar to bring them back
to an awareness of the Supernal Oneness or its inescapable sovereignty over all creation. But what seems to have been most clearly
true of this Day of the Blowing of the Horn for Remembrance
is that it was both connected with and preparatory to Yom Ha-
Kippurim, the Day of Atonement.

But what was atonement in biblical times, and how did the
ancient Israelites prepare for it? Atonement was a moral and spiritual purification, and the ancient Israelites believed that there were
three ritual occasions that possessed an almost magical capacity
to effect atonement: (1) the propitiatory sacrifices one made at
the Great Temple, (2) the day of Yom Kippur, and (3) death itself.
But as powerful as these occasions were, none of them could

bring about atonement without the prerequisite of a verbal con-fession — an acknowledgment of the precise nature of our im-purity spoken out loud. A Vidui — a confession of sin — had to be recited as we offered the propitiatory sacrifices; it had to be recited on Yom Kippur; and it had to be recited on the deathbed as well. This recitation activated the considerable power each of these moments possessed. If there was no Vidui, this power was lost. Awareness made this power actual and active in the world.

Atonement still works this way, even though we no longer make propitiatory sacrifices. It is still the case that in order for Yom Kippur to effect atonement for us, we have to find a way from unconsciousness to consciousness; we have to become aware of our moral and spiritual condition; we have to become aware that we are not operating in a spiritual vacuum — that there is, in fact, a transcendent consciousness out there watching us with unbear-able compassion as we blunder through the world. Moreover, we have to become aware of the precise nature of our blunders. The Day of Remembrance, or the Day of the Blowing of the Horn for Remembrance (or the Day of Mindfulness, for the Hebrew root *zakar*, as in Yom Ha-Zikaron, suggests both remembrance and mindfulness), was the day when we began to cultivate such an awareness. So it was that by talmudic times, Rosh Hashanah had become, above all, Yom Ha-Din, the Day of Judgment, the day when we began to see ourselves through the eyes of a conscious-ness beyond us. But it was not a final judgment. This judgment always stood *in relation to* Yom Kippur, the Day of Atonement; it could always be atoned for. "All are judged on Rosh Hashanah and the verdict is sealed on Yom Kippur," says the Tosefta, an early

—

compendium of talmudic teachings. The Babylonian Talmud gave this idea flesh and bones in the following story:

> Three books are opened on Rosh Hashanah, one for the completely evil, one for the completely righteous, and one for everyone in between. The completely righteous are written and sealed in the Book of Life immediately. The completely evil are written and sealed in the Book of Death immediately. Those in between stand suspended from Rosh Hashanah until Yom Kippur. If they merit it, they are written for life. If they do not merit it, they are written for death.

How did one come to merit being written in the Book of Life?

> Four things will cause God to tear up [ma'akirin] the decree of judgment which has been issued against a person: acts of righteousness, fervent prayer, changing one's name, and changing one's behavior.

There are echoes of these two talmudic sources in the liturgical high point of both the Rosh Hashanah and Yom Kippur services, the Une Tane Tokef prayer:

> On Rosh Hashanah it is written, and on Yom Kippur it is sealed, who will live and who will die . . . but Teshuvah [returning, turning, repentance], Prayer, and Righteous Deeds can transform [ma'avirin] the evil of the decree.

—

The liturgy is obviously derived from the talmudic story about the three books. Both claim that righteous deeds, prayer, and turning (changing one's behavior in the first case, and Teshuvah in the second) will modify the Divine Decree that has been issued on Rosh Hashanah, but the operative verbs are strikingly different. The Talmud claims that these activities will actually cause the decree to be torn up (*ma'akirin*). That which was decreed to happen will not in fact happen. The liturgy, however, makes a very different claim, namely that prayer, righteousness, and Teshuvah will not change what *happens* to us; rather, they will change *us*. We will understand what happens differently. These activities will not tear up the decree; rather, they will transform (*ma'avirin*) the evil of the decree. Spiritual practice won't change what happens. Rather, it will help us to experience what happens not as evil, but simply as what happens. Spiritual practice will help us to understand that everything that happens, even the decree of death, flows from God.

This difference of one little verb represents an immense theological sea change, a thousand years in the making. It took approximately that long for Jews to notice that there were people in their midst who spent the ten days between Rosh Hashanah and Yom Kippur praying fiercely, performing righteous deeds until they collapsed in exhaustion, repenting prodigiously and with unassailable sincerity, but who nevertheless died during the following year. In fact there were people who behaved this way all year long and still died. So when the Torah spoke of atonement, and the Talmud spoke of tearing up the divine decree, obviously they were not talking about something that took place in the visible world. They were talking about an invisible process. They

—

were talking about a spiritual process. They were talking about transformation.

But while this realization solved the most pressing theological problems rather nicely, it also upped the spiritual ante considerably. Could this kind of transformation realistically be achieved in ten days? Of course not! We were no longer talking about an act of propitiatory magic like animal sacrifice; now we were talking about something real, something that took time, and something that had an authentic rhythm and span of its own and could not be hurried. And so began the layering on of ritual. The process of transformation began to expand from what originally occupied ten days to what now takes just over two months, stretching out into a period of time long enough to hold the journey the soul had to make. The period of preparation became both longer and more complex, being divided eventually into several components. And we began to see the Days of Awe as stretching beyond themselves as well, concluding not with the great closing of the gate at the end of Yom Kippur, as they used to do, but extending out to the end of Sukkot, nearly two weeks later. Moreover, it became clear that this was a process that never ended, that rather it stretched out to the infinite horizon. These two months merely stood for something that was going on all the time. The business of transformation was going on all the time. It never stopped. The two-month period in question was merely a time when we focused on it, when we gave form to something invisible that lay dormant yet was possible to awaken at every moment of our lives.

So the walls of our great house are crumbling all the time, and not just in midsummer at Tisha B'Av, when we mourn the destruction of the Temple. Every moment of our lives, the sacred house of our life — the constructs by which we live and to which we hold on so fiercely — nevertheless falls away. Every moment, we take in a breath and the world comes into being, and then we let out a breath and the world falls away. Every moment, we experience what we take to be death, loss, and failure. When we become aware that this is happening, we feel dislocated, uprooted, filled with sorrow and anxiety. We feel estranged from our own lives, and we realize how much these constructs have been keeping us from the reality of our lives — how we have been using them to give us distance from the gnawing suspicion that we have no house — that we are afloat in a great sea of being, an endless flow of becoming in which we are connected to all beings. The great journey of transformation begins with the acknowledgment that we need to make it. It is not something we are undertaking for amusement, nor even for the sake of convention; rather, it is a spiritual necessity.

And our need to be more conscious — to awaken from the deep dream that has held us in its thrall — is always there too, not just when the shofar blows on the first day of Elul. The soul wants to awaken. Every day we are called to the present moment of our lives. Every moment we feel ourselves falling out of real time and back into the dream, but then the horn blows and we begin to return to life once again.

And this awakening is always a matter of the utmost urgency, not just in that last week before Rosh Hashanah, at Selichot. It is always something very real for which we are completely unprepared.

And the time of transformation is always upon us. The world is always cracking through the shell of its egg to be born.

—

The gate between heaven and earth is always creaking open. The Book of Life and the Book of Death are open every day, and our name is written in one or the other of them at every moment, and then erased and written again the moment after that. We are constantly becoming, continuously redefining ourselves. This doesn't just happen on Rosh Hashanah.

And every day of our life is fraught with meaning and dread, not just the Ten Days of Teshuvah. We always live at an unbearable nexus. Everything we do, every prayer we utter, every intention we form, every act of compassion we perform, always ripples out from the center of our being to the end of time. We always stand at the end of a long chain of consequences as well, and we are always struggling to control things that won't submit to our control, personal outcomes that were set in motion long ago.

And there is always a trial going on, not just the heavenly court that convenes at Kol Nidre on the eve of Yom Kippur. We are called to judgment at every moment. Our response to every moment is a judgment on us, one that is continuously unfolding, and subject to continuous modification.

And every moment is a rehearsal for our death. From the day we are born, we are engaged in the process of dying, not only because the larger arc of our life is moving in that direction, but because we experience death moment by moment. We die to the world every time we breathe out, and every time we breathe in, every time our breath returns to us of its own accord, we are reborn, and the world rises up into being again.

And our heart is always breaking, and the gate is always clanging shut. It is always the last minute. We are always desperate, not just at Neilah, the final moments of Yom Kippur. And the houses we live in never afford us real security. Their walls and roofs are never complete — they never really keep us from the world or from harm, and it is only when we realize this that we are truly home. And the task of finding an authentic source of security falls to us all the time, not just on Sukkot, when we leave our houses and go and sit in an imaginary house with the wind in our hair and the stars shining down on the top of our head.

So this concatenation of ritual — this dance that begins on Tisha B'Av and ends on Sukkot, that begins with the mournful collapse of a house and ends with the joyful collapse of a house, this intentional spasm that awakens us and carries us through death and back to life again — stands for the journey the soul is always on. It is a map, drawn by the soul, of the journey it must take, of the journey it is already taking. Beginning from the barest of biblical outlines, the soul has filled in this map with its own imperatives.

Our souls are making this journey, yours and mine.

The trip will go better for us if we know where we're going.

CHAPTER TWO

Everywhere He Went,
He Was Heading
for Home

Teshuvah

Before we begin this journey, before we walk this map of the soul step by step, let's first step back and take a look at the essential gesture of the journey; the single, consistent movement that characterizes it from start to finish. I am speaking here of Teshuvah, a Hebrew word that we struggle to translate. We call it repentance. We call it return. We call it a turning. It is all of these things and none of these things. It is a word that points us to the realm beyond language, the realm of pure motion and form.

One summer my wife, Sherril, and I took a white-water rafting trip. We were out on the Rogue River in western Oregon for three straight days, and the experience was so intense that it engraved itself on my mind very deeply.

—

For the rest of the week, I saw the river whenever I closed my eyes — the banks rolling by as we were carried inexorably toward the end of the day. I even began to dream of the river, and I realized that the reason this image stayed with me so powerfully was because it was already there. Those three days on the river had dredged up one of my deepest atavistic memories, the image of a voyage down a river, the banks of time rolling by as we head toward home, now over dangerous rapids, now over still waters, now at a leisurely float, now at a lightning plunge, but always moving, always homeward bound toward the sea.

Yet this journey home is a curious one. Rivers only run one way. The home we leave to begin this journey is necessarily a different place than the home we arrive at in the end. Abraham, the first Jew, whose nickname, Ha-Ivri, may very well have meant "the one who crossed the river," began his biblical journey by leaving the home of his birth — his father's house, the land he was born in — and setting out for an unknown land. This unknown land was his real home, the home God had destined him for. And the Children of Israel had to leave Egypt — the birthplace in which they had never felt at home — and undertake a forty-year journey across the wilderness to their real home, a place none of them had ever seen.

But here is the $64,000 question: Why do these biblical figures all have to leave home in order to find a home in order to leave again? More to the point, why do we?

Why do we have to leave our home to find a home, and then leave again? I think this is a profoundly Jewish question, not just because we are wanderers, a people destined to live without a true home for close to two thousand years while somehow managing to hold on to our identity, but also because the Jewish sacred calendar — the sacred year — embodies the essential paradox of this homeward journey. Nowhere is this more evident than during the months surrounding the High Holidays, that quarter of the year that begins in midsummer with the observance of Tisha B'Av — the day when we mourn the destruction of the Temple — then moves through the High Holidays themselves, a period of intense self-revelation and purification, and ends with Sukkot, the time of our great rejoicing, when we erect a house that is not really a house, a home that is not really a home, a time when we seem to have come to the end of a journey only to begin it again.

My earliest dreams as a child in Brooklyn, New York, were all of being lost — of not being able to find my way home. I would be walking through towering and unfamiliar urban canyons, searching for a sign of home and finding none. I remember waking from these dreams in a sweat, and not knowing where I was.

In 1970, at the age of twenty-six, I came to live in Gualala, California. There I continued to dream of my lost home. In this version of the dream, I had been taken captive by a huge man with a fez, a shaven head, and bare arms. He took me back to a small apartment crammed full of books on the arcane sciences and strapped me into a chair. Then he pulled a lever and I died. I remember saying to myself in the dream, "You can't die in a dream!" but I died nevertheless. I remember the cold horror I felt as everything went black. But then I was reborn; my inert consciousness slowly came back to life, slowly filled with a vague, misty light that got progressively clearer and more articulated — and then, there I was. It was 1955 in White Plains, New York, a time and place of nearly perfect order and tranquillity. The world

—

was in perfect balance. American culture was still intact. There were eight baseball teams in each league. The Brooklyn Dodgers had just won the World Series. Rounded cars without tail fins were parked on a sunny street lined with rosebushes full of red roses.

Why did I have that dream precisely then and there? It seems obvious to me now. There has never been a time or a place in either my life or the life of the culture when there was such an acute sense of dislocation, of having been wrenched out of one's psychic home, as there was in Gualala, California, circa 1970. American social life was in chaos, revolution was in the air, my marriage was collapsing, and the San Andreas Fault went right through my backyard. There was a gaping crater about forty feet wide between the north and south ends of my property in Gualala, left over from the big one in 1906. My favorite activity in those days was to go down to the middle of the big redwood forest where the North and South Forks of the Gualala River converged, about a mile before the river ran into the sea. I used to sit at this place for hours, watching the currents of these two channels collide. They would wrap around each other in shifting spirals and then shoot off together toward the ocean, joined now in a single, swirling flow. I was mesmerized by this place, the fluidity of it. It was a place of almost perfect instability, constant, swirling change. I tried to draw it. I tried to write music that expressed this motion, poetry about how that movement felt inside my soul. But I couldn't capture it. It eluded me. There was nothing to grab hold of. And this was true of my life then too. I couldn't get hold of it. It was eluding me. There was nothing to grab on to. No wonder I had that dream of a perfect home.

—

The dream of the lost home must be one of the deepest of all human dreams. Certainly it is the most ancient dream of the Jewish people, embodied in our national resolve to someday rebuild the Bayit — the Home — the Great Temple in Jerusalem. And this dream is the basis of that most profound expression of the American psyche, the game of baseball, a game whose object is to leave home in order to return to it again, transformed by the time spent circling the bases. And that famous shortstop Odysseus also played this game, propelled around the world by the same dream, of returning home in the end, transformed by the journey and healed by it as well.

And the truth is, every time we come home, home is different, and so are we. My mother still lives in the house near White Plains where we moved when I was seven. It is almost unbearable to go back to my old room there. All my old books are still on the bookshelf, and the oil painting of saxophonist Charlie Parker still hangs over my desk, but I feel like a ghost there — not at home in the home I grew up in any longer, but haunted everywhere else by the grid that home left in my psyche and the differential between that grid and wherever else I happen to find myself at the moment.

Some years ago I returned to the Bay Area after an absence of ten years. The move was very much motivated by a dream of return — the dream of returning to my adopted home. But home was different now. A hundred times, I had a profoundly dislocating experience while going down a street in San Francisco, in Oakland, in Berkeley. The street would seem familiar to me — intimately familiar — but subtly altered also, and I was disoriented by both the change and the familiarity.

—

We spend most of our lives, I think, in this strange dance — pushing forward to get back home. Teshuvah — turning, return, repentance — is the central gesture of the High Holiday season. It is a circular motion, Rabbi Joseph Solevetchik wrote in *On Teshuvah*, his classic work on the Days of Awe. If you are moving along the circumference of a circle, it might seem at first as if the starting point is getting farther and farther away, but actually it is also getting closer and closer. The calendar year is such a circle. On Rosh Hashanah, a new year begins, and every day is one day farther from the starting point; but every day is also a return, a drawing closer to the completion of the cycle. The biblical Prophet Samuel served the people of Israel in circuit every year. Every year, he went from Ramah to Beth El to Gilgal to Mitzpeh and then finally back to Ramah again. "The moment he left Ramah, he was already returning there," Rabbi Solevetchik pointed out. "Everywhere he went, he was heading for home."

This is not our usual sense of time. Ordinarily we see time as running in a straight line. But Rabbi Solevetchik put his finger on how time really flows. What we call Teshuvah is a primal gesture — a primordial sense of the healing power of the journey we make through life — the time spent circling the bases. Numbers express this in their natural and universal urge to return to 1 after 10.

We see this urge also in what psychiatrists call the repetition compulsion, the unconscious craving to master the unresolved elements of our life. According to this theory, we never leave the age at which trauma occurs. We keep returning, trying to move past it, to break through. If we don't, we inflict it on our children. So it is that we read in the papers of a parent who beats his children, and

—

then it comes out that this father had been beaten when he was a child. We hear the story of a mother who was shamed into dropping out of school at age fourteen, and we are shocked to learn that she is now pressuring her own teenage daughter into full-time work. In fact it is precisely these unresolved elements that cause us to return. Solevetchik wrote:

When man sins he creates a distance between himself and God. To sin means to remove oneself from the presence of the Master of the Universe. I was standing before you and Sin came and estranged me from you and I no longer feel that I am "before You." The whole essence of the precept of repentance is longing, yearning, pining to return again. Longing develops only when one has lost something precious. Sin pushes us far away and stimulates our longing to return. . . . This is why Rambam wrote: How powerful is repentance, for it brings man closer to the presence of God.

So Tisha B'Av, the day when we remember our estrangement from God, is the beginning of the process of Teshuvah. This very estrangement is the engine that drives us on our journey back home, back to God.

One spring, in the course of my pastoral rounds, I became extremely fond of a young woman named Sonya. I was visiting her during a bout with cancer that eventually took her life. She was a brilliant, open person whose deep sense of spirituality only grew considerably deeper as her illness progressed. This woman had a very difficult relationship with her mother, and this difficulty had created a distance between them which even her illness could not overcome. Her mother lived in another city. She came to the area several times on business when her daughter was in the hospital, but she didn't come to see her then. Toward the end of her illness, Sonya's mind began to slip. She had been a brilliant mathematician, but now she had difficulty expressing even the simplest thoughts. One unforgettable afternoon when I came to see her, there was something she really needed to tell me — a story, actually — and she summoned all her concentration in order to do it. It seemed terribly important to her that she tell me this story. She made everyone else leave the room before she began, and she shooed away two doctors and several close friends who tried to come into the room before she was finished.

This was the story. The week before, two friends had visited to give her an extremely deep massage, both of them working on her at once. As ill as she was, she began to experience sensations of pleasure such as she had never experienced before. Then, suddenly, a deeply buried memory burst upon her. It was a memory of her mother. Her mother was very young, perhaps twenty or twenty-one, and Sonya herself was just an infant, perhaps two, perhaps even younger. Her mother was gazing down at her with a look of absolutely pure and intense love, as if Sonya were the most beautiful thing her mother had ever seen, and that was the way her mother looked to Sonya as well.

That was the starting point, Sonya said.

What did she mean by this? Did she mean that this moment of pure feeling — of pure love — was the starting point, the basis of all the relationships she would have later on in her life? Or did she mean that it could become the beginning of a reconciliation with her mother now? Or did it mean that this memory was something essential, something she could hold on to and possibly even take with her through the difficult crossing that lay ahead? I had an urgent need to know what she meant — as urgent as her own need to tell me this story had been, but it was too late. She couldn't tell me any more. It had taken her last ounce of concentration to tell me the story, and now she had nothing left at all. She fell into incoherence, and then a deep, deep sleep. We never spoke again.

A short while later I read a newspaper story about Dwight Gooden, the baseball player. Dwight Gooden had just come back from the dead, so to speak. After one of the most brilliant beginnings in the history of baseball, Gooden's career had gone down in a maelstrom of premature fame, drug involvement, and denial. Then he righted himself — beat his problem, matured as a human being, returned to baseball, and even to New York to pitch again, this time for the Yankees. And after a period of struggle, he found his way back to a rhythm of sorts and became a capable pitcher for the Yankees. There was always about him the weight of his lost potential, what he could have become but did not, but there were flashes of his early brilliance too, and finally he pitched the first no-hitter of his career. His father, whose heart had ached to see Gooden suffer so after such a brilliant beginning, now lay dying in a hospital in St. Petersburg, Florida. The day after the no-hitter, Dwight Gooden flew back home to Florida to give his father the ball he had pitched it with. He said he owed it to his father, for all the days when he was a kid and his father would take him out to the fields to throw a ball back and forth with him.

I think one of the things we learn in the course of the long journey home is to keep our eye on the ball, on the starting point,

—

on the things in life that are essential, that sustain us. One of the ways our lives heal us is to teach us this.

Judaism believes in the particularity of time, that certain times have special spiritual properties: that Shabbat has an extra degree of holiness; that Pesach (Passover) is the time of our liberation; that Shavuot is a time unusually conducive to revelation. But they have these special properties only when we are mindful. If we consciously observe Shabbat, Shabbat has this holy quality. If we don't, it is merely Friday night, merely Saturday afternoon. And when it is invested with our awareness, Yom Kippur, the day itself, has the power to heal, to atone.

Our tradition makes precisely the same claim for death. Death, the only other time in our life when we recite the Vidui, when we bring ourselves to the point of full awareness, also atones. Death, the destination of our journey through life, also heals. Teshuvah is the little death that connects us to the big one. Or as the Rambam says: The repentant should change his name, as if to say, I am another. I am not the same person who did these deeds. It is as if that person has died. This is why this day resembles a dress rehearsal for our death.

There is a story about Alfred Nobel, the inventor of dynamite. One day his older brother died, and a newspaper got the story wrong and printed Alfred's obituary instead. Alfred opened the paper that morning and had the unusual experience of reading his obituary while he was still alive. "Dr. Alfred Nobel, who became rich by finding ways to kill more people faster than ever before, died yesterday," the obituary began. Alfred threw down the paper. That's not how I want to be remembered, he said. That's

—

not what's important to me, he said, and right then and there he decided to throw his entire fortune into rewarding people for bettering this world and bringing it closer to peace.

Yom Kippur is the day we all get to read our own obituary. It's a dress rehearsal for our death. That's why we wear a kittel, a shroudlike garment, on this day; why we refrain from life-affirming activities such as eating, drinking, and procreating. We are rehearsing the day of our death, because death, like Yom Kippur, atones.

And what our tradition is affirming with these claims is the healing power of time. What our tradition is affirming is that when we reach the point of awareness, everything in time — everything in the year, everything in our life — conspires to help us. Everything becomes the instrument of our redemption.

The banks of the river roll by. We leave home to return home. Loss is inevitable. Entropy is a fact of life. What's done cannot be undone — but it can be healed; it can even become the instrument of our healing. The year rolls by with all its attendant loss and failure, death and disappointment, but at the end of the year there is a day that heals. Life rolls by, and the same is true of the end of life as well.

The passage of time brings awareness, and the two together, time and consciousness, heal. The voyage between death and birth, between the home we come from and the home at the end of our voyage, is a journey of healing. This is precisely the journey we take every year during the High Holidays — a journey of transformation and healing, a time which together with consciousness heals and transforms us.

—

And the urge to return, that primal impulse buried deep in our psyche, is the current that propels us down this river. It is this impulse that launches the healing process.

We see this not only in the course of the year or the course of our lives. We can see this every moment of our lives as well. Every moment of our lives our suffering, our clinging to our lives, drives us out of our lives — away from home — and every moment, our awareness brings us back — returns us to ourselves, because we need to return, need to come back.

Consciousness and the passage of time heal. Loss is inevitable, but as time passes, what we really have and who we really are begins to become clear. The world of illusion begins to lose its power over us as we approach the world of truth. The thrall of the material world begins to lose its hold on us and the objects in our life begin to fall away, and it becomes increasingly clear that those things which are the least solid — the least material, the least substantial — last the longest, have the greatest effect, and in the end are the only things we leave behind.

Rabbi Laura Geller tells of a visit she once made to her ninety-five-year-old grandmother at an old-age home in Boston. Her grandmother, a beautiful woman with perfectly smooth skin and radiant eyes, had obviously taken great care in dressing and making herself up to look good for her granddaughter. Rabbi Geller had brought pictures of her family to show her: the great-grandchildren her grandmother barely knew, a husband she had only met a few times. But the time passed very quickly, and far too soon it was time to go. As Rabbi Geller stood to leave, her grandmother said, "I want to give you something. What can I give you?" Her world had become continuously smaller as she aged. She had outlived her husband, all of her siblings, most of her friends, and even a grand-child. She had moved from a lovely home to a spacious apartment to a single room in a nursing home. All of her furniture and most of her chattels had long since been distributed to her grandchildren. What was there left to give? Rabbi Geller writes:

With great ceremony, she signaled her aide to open the top drawers and bring forward a box. In it were several silk scarves, once beautiful, but now yellowed with age. "Here," she said. "I want you to have these." I started to protest that I didn't wear scarves, but suddenly I understood. She just wanted me to take something of her with me, back to my life so far away in California, back to those great-grandchildren she barely knew. She wanted to accompany me in some way, protect me like she used to when I was little, and she wanted to make sure I would remember her after she was gone.

Rabbi Geller's grandmother was a woman well healed by life. The passage of time had reduced her to her essential nature, and this is what she had passed on to her granddaughter in the form of a worn scarf. Little by little her house and then all her possessions had been stripped away. Little by little her life had carried her home — returned her to a sense of what was most important.

It takes the living of a whole life — a life and a death, the complete journey — to learn that. We are all making that journey, and the High Holidays are a dress rehearsal for it, a time when we are all stripped down — a time that gives us an intimation of what this long, strange journey home is all about.

—

The passage of time, another year — like our life, like our death — heals us, carries us toward home, makes us whole, gives us a sense of what is important in life. One spring I took my elder daughter, Hannah, away for a little vacation. It had been a very hard year for her — a hard year for the whole family — and I thought it would be good if we spent a few days alone together. Someone had offered us their summer house in Sebastopol to stay in, so we went there. Only after we'd arrived did it occur to us that Hannah had been born in Sebastopol and had lived there for the first two years of her life. I showed her the house we used to live in. The next morning we drove out to the coast along the Russian River, as my wife and I had done so often when she was pregnant with Hannah. We drove past the inn where Hannah had been conceived on our wedding night, where my wife had dreamed that we were driving through the stars in an old pickup truck and we stopped to pick Hannah up.

Then we drove up the coast to Gualala, and I found myself heading straight for that spot in the redwoods where the North and South Forks of the Gualala River converge. Hannah and I got out of the car and stood together by this spot, watching the currents swirl together. The water was green and blue and brown. Each pebble beneath our feet was distinct, had been brought there by the movements of the current — by chance and destiny and design. And I realized that if I had never lived here with my first wife, then the next thing in my life would not have happened, nor the next, nor any of the other things that led me to my present life — which had made me whole. Which had healed me.

—

And I realized something else. Something astonishing. This place we were standing in, this completely fluid place — this place of endlessly swirling currents with nothing to hold on to, nothing solid or substantial about it, this place made of water and light and movement — this was my home. I had come home.

Standing in that river I could feel all the loss in my life — all the people I had loved who were no longer there, all the people I loved now who were slipping away, all the things I had hoped for myself and my family which hadn't happened and which I now realized never would. But I could also feel the strength and the love that had come in the wake of this loss.

And in this place, it was healing to feel all that — there was a fluid sense of wholeness. I had come home. I had made Teshuvah. I could feel the transforming power of the time spent circling the bases.

Rabbi Solevetchik said of the Prophet Samuel that although he belonged to all of Israel, his true home was only in one place, Ramah. Although he led and judged in many different places, the force of his leadership and judgment stemmed from Ramah, from his home. "No matter how great a person may be, he cannot leave his real home. All of his judgments are derived from there."

Our home is a river, a fluid place, a place where there is no stopping point — a place where we can stop clinging, and stop being driven out of life. A place of Teshuvah, a place that will return us to ourselves, where we can feel our lives flowing, healing, toward home.

We all live in such a river. Each of the years of our life is a river, and our life as a whole is a river as well. And every pebble

—

beneath our feet is distinct, has been brought here by the movement of the current, by chance and destiny and design.

The day of Yom Kippur itself atones. The journey through time which surrounds it heals. If you open yourself to them, these Holy Days carry you home.

—

CHAPTER THREE

I Turned,
the Walls Came Down,
and There I Was

Tisha B'av

The soul is always teetering between two great tidal pulls: the sun and the moon, the conscious and the unconscious, the mind and the heart. In Judaism — in Jewish ritual — this invisible reality is made visible in various ways. First of all, the Hebrew calendar is the only one in the world that is both lunar and solar. The Roman calendar, which the western world still follows, is utterly unconscious of the moon. The full moon might occur at the beginning of the month, at the end of it, or in its middle — it's a nonevent in the Roman calendar. All of a sudden we look up and the moon is full or new or half-full. Unless we are fishermen or farmers, we are caught utterly by surprise. In lunar calendars, on the other hand, it is the revolution of

---

the earth around the sun that is ignored. The Muslim calendar, for example, is lunar, and Ramadan floats happily across the solar year, appearing in autumn one year and in midwinter the next, and in the spring the year after that.

Every Hebrew month follows the cycles of the moon quite precisely. Each new moon is Rosh Chodesh, a minor religious holiday, and most of the major holidays occur on the full moon. But the years follow the cycle of the sun also, albeit with somewhat less precision. We simply throw in an extra month every couple of years (we call this process intercalation), and this ensures that the Jewish year will never be more than a week or two out of phase with the earth's revolution around the sun. So we feel both the sun and the moon in our lives. We feel the phases of the moon tugging at our hearts and our groins, and the progress of the earth through its phases — from summer to autumn and from winter to spring. This bipolar tidal pull is also reflected in Judaism by the two great yearly spiritual cycles that run in parallel revolutions from one High Holiday season to the next: the sacred calendar and the weekly cycle of Torah readings.

The sacred calendar begins each year at Rosh Hashanah, and continues through Yom Kippur, Sukkot, Hanukkah, Purim, Pesach, Shavuot, and then finally Tisha B'Av. This cycle of festivals carries us from spiritual purification to gratitude and joy; from spiritual renewal to liberation and then to revelation; from the fullness of the year, and its attendant decline and death, to a pageant of renewal and rebirth. The reading of the Torah has a yearly cycle as well. The entire Torah is read in approximately equal weekly portions every year. On Simchat Torah, the climactic moment of the fall holiday season, the yearly cycle of Torah readings

is both completed and begun again in a single reading. The last
letter of the Torah is the letter lamed, or L (the last letter of the
Torah's final word, *Yisrael*). The first letter of the Torah is beit, or
B (the first letter in the word *Bereshit*, "In the beginning").
Together, these two letters are themselves a word, the word *lev*,
the Hebrew word for heart. If the sacred calendar traces the path
of the soul, then the Torah is the path of the heart. It is, in fact, the
heart that keeps the sacred calendar going, that joins its end to
its beginning.

But just as the sun and the moon feel each other tugging at
the surface of the earth and on its seas, just as each of their pulls
affects the other, so the sacred calendar and the yearly cycle of
Torah readings affect each other too. They often rhyme in subtle
ways; they use the same language or address the same issues at the
same time. Pesach, for example, is the holiday of physical purification. We get down to essentials. We remove all leaven — all
flour that has undergone modification and expansion — from our
homes and then finally from our bodies. We possess and we eat
only the essence of the flour, the unrisen wheat. And we get rid of
that which is stale — all the old flour in our possession. And what
do we read in the Torah during the weeks when we are preparing
for this purification? The laws concerning the cult of purification
at the Great Sanctuary in the wilderness. Similarly, Hanukkah
is the celebration of a particular kind of renewal. The ancient
Hasmoneans (also called the Maccabees), who had flirted with
the idea of assimilating into Hellenist culture, experience an
awakening of sorts — a heroic rededication to the imperatives of
the Jewish spiritual impulse. Meanwhile, in the Torah we are reading the story of Joseph, who rose to power in Egypt, took an

—

Egyptian name, took an Egyptian wife, dressed like an Egyptian, and denied his Jewish brothers both to himself and to his Egyptian patrons. Finally, however, Joseph experienced an awakening, a moment when he realized at last who he was, who he had been all along, and who his brothers really were.

There is a similar rhyme between the tidal pull of the Torah-reading cycle and the pull of the sacred calendar around Tisha B'Av. Tisha B'Av is a day associated with the various calamities that have befallen the Jewish people since the earliest days of their history, particularly the destruction of the two Great Temples of Jerusalem. The First Temple was destroyed by Nebuchadnezzar and the Babylonians on the ninth day of the month of Av. The Second Temple was destroyed by the Romans on the same date in the year 70 of the Common Era. The Great Temple of Jerusalem was the navel of the universe, the earthly locus where Israel felt its connection to the Divine Presence in a palpable way. So Tisha B'Av is primarily about the loss of this connection and the calamity that comes in the wake of this loss. Tisha B'Av always coincides with the beginning of our reading from the Book of Deuteronomy.

Deuteronomy — the second telling — consists for the most part of the repetition of stories and laws we have already heard earlier in the Torah. The first story it tells is the story of a calamity. In the Book of Numbers, when the Children of Israel first arrived at the boundary of the Promised Land, God commanded them to scout out the land and then to go up and take it. But the scouts came back full of fear (of the inhabitants of the land? of the impending battle with them? of the prospect of being free and having power at last? The Torah is ambiguous on this point). They

—

conveyed their fear to the people, and the people refused to go up and take the land. This refusal became the source of a considerable estrangement between God and Israel. God brought a terrible plague on the Israelites, and it took forty years of wandering in the desert before they would have another opportunity to enter the Promised Land. Now, as the Book of Deuteronomy opens and the Children of Israel again stand on the brink of opportunity, Moses retells them that story.

אֲ

According to the Mishnah, the oldest strata of the Talmud, on Tisha B'Av we mourn not just the destruction of the Temple, but the whole series of calamities that took place both long before and long after that; we also mourn the scouts who were commanded to lead the people into the Promised Land but who brought back a misleading report and frightened the people out of going there. We read this story twice, once in Numbers, and again in Deuteronomy, and these two accounts frame the forty years wandering in the wilderness. We also mourn the fall of Betar, the climactic battle in the unsuccessful revolution against Rome that was waged a century and a half later, and the ploughing over of the Temple Mount by the Romans at the end of this war.

But these were only the calamities that the rabbis of the talmudic era were able to associate with this date. Calamities continued to occur at this time of year and they all became part of the Tisha B'Av mythos. There was an expulsion from England in the thirteenth century, a fifteenth-century expulsion from Spain, and the various massacres connected with the Crusades. Even the assassination of the Archduke Francis Ferdinand at Sarajevo, the event

—

that precipitated World War I, took place on the ninth day of the month of Av. While this was not a specifically Jewish calamity, some historians see it as the precipitating event of the Holocaust. The Pale of Settlement on the western edge of what became the Soviet Union, where the overwhelming majority of Eastern European Jews lived, became the battleground for World War I. Millions of Jews were displaced by this war, and their displacement left them sitting ducks for the events of World War II. To be sure, tragedy was constantly befalling the Jewish people before and after their exile from Israel, and one could probably compile a similar list to correspond to any time of the year. But the destruction of the Temple and the exile it occasioned were signal calamities, and the tendency to telescope calamities around this date served to give form to a significant spiritual feeling, the sense that the same thing was happening over and over again but in slightly different form, and the corresponding feeling that our unresolved tendencies — the unconscious wrong turns we keep taking — carry us back to the same point on our spiritual path again and again.

The Hebrew name for the Book of Deuteronomy is Devarim. The opening words of this book are *Eleh devarim* — "These are the words." The Book of Deuteronomy literally consists of the words of Moses; it is a first-person narration spoken by Moses, his personal version of events and ideas. The rabbis of the Talmud called this book the Mishnah Torah — the Repetition of the Law. There is very little in the way of new material in this book. Rather it is for the most part a rehashing of stories and ideas we heard earlier in the Torah, only this time we hear them from Moses himself rather than from an omniscient third-person narrator.

—

Moses begins with a highly subjective retelling of the incident of the scouts we read about in the Book of Numbers. Why does he begin by repeating this material? Because that moment has clearly repeated itself. Once again Moses and the Children of Israel stand at a moment of transformation; once again they stand at the edge of the Promised Land with an opportunity to go up and take it. The last time they stood at this point, this moment of opportunity, they failed to seize it, and they became alienated from God and began a protracted period of exile as a consequence.

Now they are being given a second chance. Forty years before, they stood on exactly the same spot, facing exactly the same situation, and now it is time to see if they have learned anything, if they can move past this experience and get on with their lives. Or if they failed to learn, will this same calamity continue to replicate itself until they do? Will the unconscious, unresolved elements in their lives that brought them back to this moment continue to do so, or will they finally get past them?

There are two ways of looking at the way our tradition has collapsed history on this day, two ways of thinking about this conflation of calamity. We can regard the ninth of Av and the weeks surrounding it as a cursed time (indeed, there is something of this idea in the prohibition of weddings during this period), or we can regard the ninth of Av as a time when we are reminded that catastrophes will keep recurring in our lives until we get things right, until we learn what we need to learn from them.

Tisha B'Av comes exactly seven weeks before Rosh Hashanah, beginning the process that culminates on Rosh Hashanah and Yom Kippur. Tisha B'Av is the moment of turning, the moment when we turn away from denial and begin to face exile and

—

alienation as they manifest themselves in our own lives — in our alienation and estrangement from God, in our alienation from ourselves and from others. Teshuvah — turning, repentance — is the essential gesture of the High Holiday season. It is the gesture by which we seek to heal this alienation and to find at-one-ment: to connect with God, to reconcile with others, and to anchor ourselves in the ground of our actual circumstances, so that it is this reality that shapes our actions and not just the habitual, unconscious momentum of our lives.

Rambam, the great medieval philosopher and synthesizer of Jewish law, said that Teshuvah, this kind of moral and spiritual turning, is only complete when we find ourselves in exactly the same position we were in when we went wrong — when the state of estrangement and alienation began — and we choose to behave differently, to act in a way that is conducive to atonement and reconciliation. But this objection was raised: What happens if the circumstances in question don't repeat themselves? How do we make complete Teshuvah then? Don't worry, the Rambam replied. They always do. The unresolved elements of our lives — the unconscious patterns, the conflicts and problems that seem to arise no matter where we go or with whom we find ourselves — continue to pull us into the same moral and spiritual circumstances over and over again until we figure out how to resolve them. They continue to carry us into harm's way until we become aware of them, conscious of them, and begin to change them. And we all have recurring motifs in the dark, unresolved corners of our lives — in the domestic unhappiness we replicate from one marriage to another, in the problems that seem to follow us from one job to the next, in all the mistakes that turn out to be the same mistake, which we make over and over.

This is why Moses begins the Book of Deuteronomy — the second telling, the Repetition of the Way — with his own version of the story of the scouts. He realizes the Israelites are in precisely the same spiritual and moral predicament they found themselves in forty years before. The unresolved issues of their lives have brought them there.

And this explains a second element that Moses' story and the tradition of Tisha B'Av have in common, and that is the strange tendency of Moses, in the first case, and the rabbis of the Talmud, in the second, to blame the people themselves for what happened.

In the original account of the scouts — the third-person narration we read in the Book of Numbers — the people were certainly not without blame. They were gullible and far too easily led into a panic. But the principal blame seemed to lie elsewhere, particularly on the perfidious and cowardly scouts, the princes of the tribes, who projected their fear onto what they saw. When they returned, they described a place far worse, far more terrifying, than the one they had actually seen. This projection incited the people to fearfulness, and finally to disobedience, to a refusal to do what they were clearly meant to do next.

But later, in Deuteronomy, Moses tells the story very differently. He shifts the blame from the exaggerated and ultimately dishonest story the spies told, to the murmuring of the people who heard the report. The people are no longer innocents, misled into disobedience. Moses subtly alters the narrative in this retelling to place the burden of guilt on them and not their princes.

—

We see precisely the same kind of thing in the Tisha B'Av story. Why was the Temple destroyed? the rabbis of the Talmud asked. Because of *sinat chinam* — gratuitous hatred; because the Jewish people had fallen into factional bickering; because they had broken up into warring cults and were busily engaged in fratricidal religious disputes, each one claiming to be the true Israel and denying the legitimacy of all the others.

Isaiah Gafni is an Israeli professor of ancient history. On holidays celebrating ancient historical events, he is frequently asked to appear on Israeli radio and TV to participate in panels with other learned commentators. On Tisha B'Av, there is invariably a commentator from the Israeli left who explains that the Temple was destroyed and Israel was conquered by the Romans because of the intolerance of the religious right of that day. Then a right-wing commentator explains that both the Temple and Israel itself fell to the Romans because of the failure of the Jewish people to unite against the enemy militarily. Then it invariably falls upon Gafni to explain that there was one reason for the fall of the Temple and one reason alone: Rome was absolutely invincible, and its huge armies were marching through the world mowing down everyone in their path, and nothing could have stopped them from taking Jerusalem, no matter how tolerant the religious right nor how unified the armies of Israel might have been.

So what were the rabbis of the Talmud talking about when they said that the Temple was destroyed by gratuitous hatred? What was Moses talking about? Why did they blame the people for what had happened, when the objective evidence of history clearly seems to exonerate them?

—

The answer is that neither the rabbis nor Moses cared a fig about history. They weren't historians; they were spiritual leaders, and spiritually, the only question worth asking about any conflict, any recurring catastrophe, is this: What is my responsibility for it? How am I complicit in it? How can I prevent it from happening again?

When things go bad, there is an enormous temptation to blame it on externals, on the evil of others, or on an unlucky turn of events. Spiritually, however, we are called to resist this temptation, no matter how strong it may be and no matter how strongly rooted in fact or reason or history it may seem.

Spiritually we are called to responsibility, to ask, What am I doing to make this recur again and again? Even if it is a conflict that was clearly thrust upon me from the outside, how am I plugging in to it, what is there in me that needs to be engaged in this conflict? Why can't I just let it slough off me like water off a duck's back, as I am able to do with so many other things?

Our power in this world is considerable, but also very circumscribed. It is only here and now, in this moment, in this place — in the present — that we can act. We cannot act in the past, we cannot act in the future, and most certainly we cannot act through someone else's experience. So from a spiritual point of view, we need to ask, What can I do here and now, in the present-tense reality of my own experience?

And that is precisely where Moses and the rabbis are trying to point the people — to their own experience, which is the only place where they are empowered to act.

Why do our relationships always fail in precisely the same way? Why do we always fall into the same kind of conflict at

—

work? Why do we always have the same arguments with our children? With our parents?

Sure, there may be plenty of evidence in the history of your life to suggest that it was always the other guy's fault. That first husband was a real schmuck. Look at what happened with his second marriage. And that guy at work you are in conflict with now is the last of the schmohegans, no doubt about it. And that guy you were in conflict with last time was also a terrible schmohawk.

But we aren't talking about history here. We are talking about our spiritual growth, and in terms of our spiritual growth, what we really need to ask is this: What is my complicity? Why do I always end up fighting with schmohawks? Why does every man I have a relationship with end up taking advantage of me? How can I make things better in the here and now of my actual experience — the only time and place in which I am empowered to act?

What is the recurring disaster in our life? What is the unresolved element that keeps bringing us back to this same moment over and over again? What is it that we keep getting wrong? What is it that we persistently refuse to look at, fail to see?

Tisha B'Av is the day on which we are reminded of the calamity that keeps repeating itself in the life of our people. And against all reason — against the overwhelming evidence of history — Moses and the rabbis insist that we are not powerless in the face of that calamity. Moses and the rabbis insist that we take responsibility for what is happening to us. Moses and the rabbis insist that we acknowledge our complicity in the things that keep happening to us over and over again.

I think that the great philosopher George Santayana got it exactly wrong. I think it is precisely those who insist on remembering history who are doomed to repeat it. For a subject with so little substance, for something that is really little more than a set of intellectual interpretations, history can become a formidable trap — a sticky snare from which we may find it impossible to extricate ourselves. I find it impossible to read the texts of Tisha B'Av, with their great themes of exile and return, and their endless sense of longing for the land of Israel, without thinking of the current political tragedy in the Middle East. I write this at a very dark moment in the long and bleak history of that conflict. Who knows what will be happening there when you read this? But I think it's a safe bet that whenever you do, one thing is unlikely to have changed. There will likely be a tremendous compulsion for historical vindication on both sides. Very often, I think it is precisely the impossible yearning for historical justification that makes resolution of this conflict seem so impossible. The Jews want vindication for the Holocaust, and for the two thousand years of European persecution and ostracism that preceded it; the Jews want the same Europeans who now give them moral lectures to acknowledge that this entire situation would never have come about if not for two thousand years of European bigotry, barbarism, and xenophobia. They want the world to acknowledge that Israel was attacked first, in 1948, in 1967, in 1973, and in each of the recent Intifadas. They want acknowledgment that they only took the lands from which they were attacked during these conflicts, and offered to return them on one and only one condition — the acknowledgment of their right to exist. When

—

47

Anwar Sadat met that condition, the Sinai Peninsula, with its rich oil fields and burgeoning settlement towns, was returned to him. And they want acknowledgment that there are many in the Palestinian camp who truly wish to destroy them, who have used the language of peace as a ploy to buy time until they have the capacity to liquidate Israel and the Jews once and for all. They want acknowledgment that they have suffered immensely from terrorism, that a people who lost six million innocents scarcely seventy years ago should not have had to endure the murder of its innocent men, women, and children so soon again. And they want acknowledgment that in spite of all this, they stood at Camp David prepared to offer the Palestinians everything they claimed to have wanted — full statehood, a capital in East Jerusalem — and the response of the Palestinians was the second Intifada, a murderous campaign of terror and suicide bombings.

And the Palestinians? They would like the world to acknowledge that they lived in the land now called Israel for centuries, that they planted olive trees, shepherded flocks, and raised families there for hundreds of years; they would like the world to acknowledge that when they look up from their blue-roofed villages, their trees and their flowers, their fields and their flocks, they see the horrific, uninvited monolith of western culture — immense apartment complexes, shopping centers, and industrial plants on the once-bare and rocky hills where the voice of God could be heard and where Muhammad ascended to heaven. And they would like the world to acknowledge that it was essentially a European problem that was plopped into their laps at the end of the last great war, not one of their own making. They would like the world to acknowledge that there has always been a kind of

—

arrogance attached to this problem; that it was as if the United States and England said to them, Here are the Jews, get used to them. And they would like the world to acknowledge that it is a great indignity, not to mention a significant hardship, to have been an occupied people for so long, to have had to submit to strip searches on the way to work, and intimidation on the way to the grocery store, and the constant humiliation of being subject — a humiliation rendered nearly bottomless when Israel, with the benefit of the considerable intellectual and economic resources of world Jewry, made the desert bloom, in a way they had never been able to do. And they would like the world to acknowledge that there are those in Israel who are determined never to grant them independence, who have used the language of peace as a ploy to fill the West Bank with settlement after settlement until the facts on the ground are such that an independent Palestinian state on the West Bank is an impossibility. They would like the world to acknowledge that there is no such thing as a gentle occupation — that occupation corrodes the humanity of the occupier and makes the occupied vulnerable to brutality.

And I think the need to have these things acknowledged — the need for historical affirmation — is so great on both sides that both the Israelis and the Palestinians would rather perish as peoples than give this need up. In fact, I think they both feel that they *would* perish as peoples precisely if they did. They would rather die than admit their own complicity in the present situation, because to make such an admission would be to acknowledge the suffering of the other and the legitimacy of the other's complaint, and that might mean that they themselves were wrong, that they were evil, that they were bad. That might give the other an

—

opening to annihilate or enslave them. That might make such behavior seem justifiable.

I wonder how many of us are stuck in a similar snare. I wonder how many of us are holding on very hard to some piece of personal history that is preventing us from moving on with our lives, and keeping us from those we love. I wonder how many of us cling so tenaciously to a version of the story of our lives in which we appear to be utterly blameless and innocent, that we become oblivious to the pain we have inflicted on others, no matter how unconsciously or inevitably or innocently we may have inflicted it. I wonder how many of us are terrified of acknowledging the truth of our lives because we think it will expose us. How many of us stand paralyzed between the moon and the sun; frozen — unable to act in the moment — because of our terror of the past and because of the intractability of the present circumstances that past has wrought? Forgiveness, it has been said, means giving up our hopes for a better past. This may sound like a joke, but how many of us refuse to give up our version of the past, and so find it impossible to forgive ourselves or others, impossible to act in the present?

Tisha B'Av is the beginning of Teshuvah, the process of turning that we hope to complete on Yom Kippur, the process of returning to ourselves and to God. And the acknowledgment of the unresolved in our lives, as a people and as individuals, is the beginning of the sacred power the Days of Awe grant us — to transform our lives in this moment when we feel the pull of both the waning moon and the setting sun; in this place, in this life, here and now.

—

The psalmist promises us, "The Guardian of those who struggle to know God never slumbers nor sleeps. He will protect you. He will not let the sun smite you by day, nor the moon by night."

צ

During the Watergate investigation, Deep Throat told reporters Bob Woodward and Carl Bernstein to "follow the money." In Torah study, the watchword is "follow the language." A given Torah portion will often convey its essential meaning by repeating a particular word or word-root (*shoresh*) a significant number of times. Three times, seven times, ten times — these are the most common magic numbers, although among these, seven is the one most frequently employed. These repeated words become a kind of leitmotiv, a theme that points us to the central action of the portion, and invites us to explore the word in question for a broader and deeper range of meanings.

In the first portion of Deuteronomy — the portion we always read the week of Tisha B'Av — the word that is repeated seven times is the root *phanah* — to turn. "*Rav lachem,*" God says.

"The time is up for living on this mountain. Turn [*ph'nu*] and begin your journey." . . . And we turned [*v'neifen*] and we passed by the way of the wilderness of Moav. . . . And we turned [*v'neifen*] and we went up to Bashan . . .

"To turn" is certainly a redolent verb. But one of the unmistakable suggestions of its repeated usage here is that the Children

—

of Israel have once again reached a significant turning point. They
stand once again at the border of the Promised Land. Once again,
life and God are conspiring to confront them with a clear and
frightening imperative. Go up and take the land. *Rav lachem* —
the time has come for this. This is what you must do next in order
for your life to proceed. This is what you must do in order to move
on to the next stage of your journey. Forty years ago, of course, the
Children of Israel resisted this imperative and did not go up, and
as a consequence their lives ground to a standstill. Now the turning point has come round again.

The calendar of the sacred year presents us with a succession
of turning points, and — *rav lachem* — each turn comes in its
own time. The number seven, the number associated with creation and light, is always connected with these turning points.
Seven weeks before Pesach, we turn toward the process of purification that will culminate during the week of Pesach itself by
celebrating Shabbat Shekalim, the first of a number of special
Sabbaths designed to draw us into this process by calling our
attention to it. Pesach itself is a turning point. It is exactly seven
weeks before Shavuot. Pesach commemorates liberation — the
exodus from Egypt — and Shavuot celebrates revelation — the
giving of the Torah on Mount Sinai. Liberation, the calendar suggests, is the great turning point on the road to revelation.

Exactly seven weeks before Rosh Hashanah, we mark the turn
toward Teshuvah — repentance or return — with the observance
of Tisha B'Av. Tisha B'Av is the beginning of Teshuvah, the point
of turning toward this process by turning toward a recognition of
our estrangement from God, from ourselves, and from others.
Yom Kippur is the culmination of the process that begins on Tisha

—

B'Av, when we acknowledge the darkness, when we let our guard down, when we turn toward the truth.

The natural event connected to Tisha B'Av is the height of summer, the fullness of the year. Six days later, on the fifteenth of Av, the summer actually reaches its peak and begins to decline; the sap in the trees reaches its full strength and begins to turn toward dryness. The days reach their full length and begin to shorten. Fullness and decline are intimately linked. The end of one is the beginning of the other. Conversely, decline and destruction necessarily precede renewal; tearing down is necessary before rebuilding is possible. And all these things — fullness, decline, destruction, renewal, tearing down, rebuilding — are actually part of the same process, points on a single continuum, consecutive segments of a never-ending circle.

The time between Tisha B'Av and Yom Kippur, this great seven-week time of turning, is the time between the destruction of Jerusalem — the crumbling of the walls of the Great Temple — and our own moral and spiritual reconstruction. The year has been building itself up, and now it begins to let go — the natural cycle of the cosmos, the rise and fall, the impermanence and the continuity, all express themselves in this turning. The walls come down and suddenly we can see, suddenly we recognize the nature of our estrangement from God, and this recognition is the beginning of our reconciliation. We can see the image of the falling Temple — the burning house — that Tisha B'Av urges upon us so forcefully, precisely in this light.

One of the extraordinary things about the Torah is the amount of time and space it devotes to the physical details of the sanctuary in the wilderness, the Great Tabernacle, the prototype

—

53

for the Great Temple of Jerusalem. Almost half the Book of Exodus — the last five weekly Torah portions of this book — is given over to a minute and repetitive description of this structure. This schema is repeated as the Children of Israel gather the necessary materials to build it, then repeated as they begin to execute the design, and then finally repeated one more time as the erection of the Tabernacle is completed. The classical commentators, who are rarely at a loss for words, make a few forced symbolic interpretations of these structural details and then fall silent as they are repeated over and over. Page after page goes by without any commentary at all, a happenstance replicated nowhere else in the Torah. The point seems to be that the Torah is not trying to teach us nor even to tell us anything here. Rather, it seems interested in simply engraving the image of the Tabernacle in our psyches, as if it were spiritually important to have this image there; as if there were something in the structure of the Tabernacle we need to impose on our own inner structure, as if we need to bring our own inner life into harmony with this design.

It has occurred to me in recent years that the Jewish calendar year does the same thing with another image, and that is the image of the fall of the Temple. It does this through a series of public fasts. On the fifteenth of Tevet, which falls in late November and December, we fast in memory of the beginning of the siege of Jerusalem. On the seventeenth of Tammuz, a midsummer month, we fast in memory of the breaching of the walls of the city of Jerusalem, toward the end of this siege. Exactly three weeks later, on the ninth of Av (Tisha B'Av), we observe a major fast — the longest and most difficult fast of the year — to remember the fall of Jerusalem and the destruction of the Temple. Then, seven

—

weeks later, and one day after Rosh Hashanah, we observe the Fast of Gedalyah. Gedalyah was the Jewish governor who presided over Israel after it had been conquered by the Babylonians. He was assassinated by Jewish zealots — disgruntled Jewish monarchists — and after his death, the Jews were cleaned out of the land of Israel and shipped off to a Babylonian exile. So the Fast of Gedalyah marks the beginning of the Jewish Diaspora — the exile.

This image, this series of fasts, tells our bodies and our souls the story of the encroachment of emptiness: the story of impermanence. There was a Great Temple, a great nation with its capital in Jerusalem, but even such seemingly unshakable institutions as these simply slipped away into the mists of history. Yet even while it stood, the Great Temple was a structure that was centered around emptiness. The Holy of Holies, the Sacred Center upon which all the elaborate structural elegance of the Temple served to focus, was primarily a vacated space. It was defined that way in the Torah. The Holy of Holies was the space no one could enter except the high priest, and even he could only enter for a few moments on Yom Kippur. If anyone else entered this place, or if the high priest entered on any other day, the charged emptiness at the Sacred Center, the powerful nothingness there, would break out on him and overwhelm him, and he would die. So Yom Kippur is, among other things, the day we enter the vacated space, even if only by proxy, the day we experience the charged emptiness at the Sacred Center.

On Tisha B'Av it is as if this emptiness has broken loose from its bounds and swallowed everything up. The Temple burns. The emptiness once confined to the center of the Temple now characterizes it completely.

—

This image touches us deeply because we are always under siege, and we are held there by our attempts to hold off the emptiness we intuit at the center of our lives. In *The Denial of Death*, Ernest Becker observed that while all sentient beings die, we humans are the only ones who know that we will die. All of our lives, according to Becker, are an accommodation to this dreaded intelligence. Terrified of this emptiness, seeing it as utter negation, we defend against it with all our might. Against the encroachment of nothingness, we fill our lives with stuff. Against the ultimate negation, we strive for success. Against the hard information that we came from nothing and end there as well, against the resulting suspicion that we might, in fact, be nothing all the while, we struggle mightily to construct an identity, but we're never quite persuaded by it. Some deep instinct keeps whispering to us that it isn't real, and the walls keep falling down, and then the city finally collapses, and the identity we have been laboring so desperately to shore up collapses along with it.

As a rabbi, as a member of a family, as a friend, I have often witnessed the crumbling of these walls. I have often seen divorce shake up people's idea of who they are. It can destroy an identity based on being a happy spouse, or uncover the emptiness we often try to hide with a relationship that was never really gratifying. If we have invested our identities in our work, if we believe we are defined by what we do, retirement or dismissal can be a devastating trauma. I have known many men who have suffered strokes or heart attacks in the months after retirement. Several have actually died. And getting fired, even from a terrible job, often leads to a debilitating depression. If we see ourselves primarily as parents, as

—

protectors of our children, then the walls can come tumbling down when our children suffer.

A woman in my congregation had poured all her life's energy into creating the perfect family. She had three children, each one more talented and brilliant than the next. The eldest was a boy, bright, handsome, and a gifted musician. She often had him play the trumpet for her dinner guests. And he often sang duets with his younger sister, the middle child, an adorable blond. They sang "Dites-Moi" from *South Pacific*. The woman herself was brilliant and beautiful as well, and she was extremely ambitious. She had come from a very poor background, and had suffered disgrace and ostracism as a child. But now her husband was a successful doctor and her children were too good to be true. She was the envy of everyone, and soon became the center of an increasingly prestigious succession of social circles. Her husband acquired famous patients, and she began to socialize with them. Her first two children were accepted at Ivy League universities. And none of this happened by accident. She had made it happen. Her husband had wanted to begin his practice in a comfortable rural community. He might have made a nice living there, but he would have been a nonentity if she hadn't insisted that he practice in a major urban center instead. And the children required constant prodding, constant pushing, constant reminding that their success and failure were a reflection on her. She was beautiful and generous, but she had a very sharp edge.

Then her son, the bright, handsome musician, had a major breakdown. He came home from college and curled up on his bed in the fetal position. When people came to visit, they asked about

—

him, and wondered why he never came out. His mother would turn beet red then, but it was far worse when he did come out. Always a quiet and rail-thin blond, he was now coarse and over-weight. He would sit in the living room in a funk, insulting his mother's visitors, several times driving them from the house. This went on for years. There was a seemingly endless succession of psy-chiatrists, mental institutions, tawdry apartments, weird encoun-ters with strangers on the streets, desperate trips to Europe and the Caribbean. In between, he would always come home. He would lie on his bed in the fetal position. He would sit in the liv-ing room and insult his mother's friends.

His mother was devastated. Her ascent up the ladder of social success came to a complete halt. Life became a humiliation for her. Social visits were a nightmare. Either there was the heavy presence of her absent son emanating from the bedroom, or her son's actual presence, coarse and angry and abusive. And then, of course, there was her son's suffering. Above and beyond the social implications of all this was the fact that she really did love her son desperately, and her son appeared to be dying of misery. She felt the walls of her world falling down all around her.

Then, after three or four years, the misery ended as suddenly and as mysteriously as it had begun. The son met a young woman. They fell in love. They married and had three children. His life regulated itself in almost every way. There was almost no trace of those years of near madness and rage. And when the smoke had cleared, it was apparent to everyone that there was no trace of his mother's hard edge anymore, no trace of her social ambitions. Her son's nightmare and his sudden, inexplicable recovery from it had softened her. The walls of her ego had crumbled. Her son had torn them down. But everyone who knew her agreed: she was the better for it. She was warmer, softer. She had a deeper sense of what was important in her life.

We spend a great deal of time and energy propping up our identity, an identity we realize at bottom is really a construct. So it is that we are always living at some distance from ourselves. We live in a fearful state of siege, trying to prop up an identity that keeps crumbling, that we secretly intuit to be empty. Then Tisha B'Av comes and the walls begin to crumble, and then the entire city collapses. But something persists — something fundamentally nameless and empty, something that remains when all else has fallen away.

Something remained when the Temple was destroyed two thousand years ago. This was perhaps the most significant turning point in Jewish history. Judaism continued without the Temple, an inconceivable possibility at the time. But the truth is that if the Temple had never been destroyed, the renewal Judaism needed so badly could never have taken place. If the walls of the Temple had never fallen down, the fundamental spiritual impulse of Judaism — the powerful emptiness at its core — may very well have been smothered.

Many years ago, in northern California, I knew a man named Moshe, and to tell you the truth I couldn't stand the guy. He was an early follower of Shlomo Carlebach, the spiritual leader and musician, and was always barefoot, always stoned, always breaking out into spontaneous dancing, and always positively oozing a very unconvincing brand of joy. I thought he was a phony, and the phoniest thing about him was the dancing and the ersatz bliss. But one summer I went to Jerusalem, and I was on the Temple Mount

—

for the observance of Tisha B'Av, and I ran into this Moshe there. Now since it was Tisha B'Av and since he was a devoted neo-Hasid who felt compelled to enter fully into the emotional imperatives of every holiday, he was not exuding joy. Rather he was allowing himself to feel the sadness of Tisha B'Av as fully as he could. And suddenly I loved the guy. Suddenly he seemed utterly sincere. I think this Moshe was a genuinely depressed individual. All that dancing and joy had been an exhausting overlay on his natural personality. But now, because of Tisha B'Av, he was allowing himself to feel depressed and he seemed completely authentic. When the walls crumbled, when the façade of fake joy fell away, he was real; he was authentically who he was, and that's why I liked him so much. Suddenly I saw him as a man at a turning point, someone who had let the siege end, who had let the walls come all the way down, who had let the city fall, someone willing to ask, Who am I really? What will be left when the walls of constructed identity come down? He was someone who had followed the ancient imperative and said, *Rav lachem* — the time has come. The time has come to get off it, to drop the mask. After all, in seven weeks we will stand before the one who sees through all masks. The time has come to turn.

So the Torah tells us seven times. *Vneifen, u-finu* — and they turned, now you turn. What is required of us at Tisha B'Av is a simple turn of mind, a turn toward consciousness, a turn away from denial, from the inertia, from the passive momentum of our lives, a turn away from those things that continue to happen unconsciously, and a conscious decision to change. A letting go, letting the walls of identity crumble, and turning toward that which remains.

—

My first congregation was in Monroe, New York, right on the edge of the Catskill Mountains. The Catskills were an important part of my family mythology. My father had spent his teenage years there. His mother ran a boardinghouse, Lew's Wayside Inn, after she was divorced from his father. My parents both worked in Catskill hotels during the summertime when they were first married and my father was struggling to get through dental school. They couldn't afford a place to live, and the help quarters were intolerable. My mother was assigned a big strapping roommate, a waitress from the Pennsylvania coal mining country. This woman was making more money entertaining gentleman callers in their room late at night than she was making in the dining room. My mother couldn't take it. She and my father ended up sleeping out in the fields together every night. It was wonderfully romantic.

My father died a few years before I became a rabbi in Monroe. The Catskills held precious memories for my mother, so one day during my first year at Monroe, about a week before Tisha B'Av, my wife and I took her on a sentimental journey to the Catskills. She would show us Lew's Wayside Inn. She would show us the hotel she had worked in that first year, and the fields where she and my father had slept. She would show us the hotel where she and my father had worked together their second summer there as well.

But when we got up to the Catskills, it was all gone. There was no trace of any of it. The first hotel had become a prison. The field where my mother and father had lain together all those summer nights was now filled to bursting with the Quonset huts and chain-link fences of a state mental hospital. The second hotel had become a yeshiva. And Lew's Wayside Inn? Who knew? The road

—

that used to lead there didn't even exist anymore. It simply stopped dead in its tracks about a half a mile before the inn, shrubs and weeds gaping out from where the roadbed used to be. By this time my mother was weeping profusely in the backseat. She wept all the way back to Monroe. Finally she came to herself. "I'm glad we went," she said. "It was important."

God knows why my mother felt it was important to witness such a relentless demonstration of the impermanence of the life she had known in the Catskills. I doubt if she could have explained what she meant by this herself. But what I took her to mean was that she understood that this was the only way she could have that life. Only by being willing to experience loss — by letting the walls of memory crumble — could she have it. This is the bet life always makes against us. Life bets that we won't be willing to endure the suffering it requires. Life bets that we will try to shut out the suffering, and so shut out life in the bargain. Tisha B'Av sidles up to us, whispering conspiratorially with a racing form over its mouth. Tisha B'Av has a hot tip for us: Take the suffering. Take the loss. Turn toward it. Embrace it. Let the walls come down.

And Tisha B'Av has a few questions for us as well. Where are we? What transition point are we standing at? What is causing sharp feeling in us, disturbing us, knocking us a little off balance? Where is our suffering? What is making us feel bad? What is making us feel at all? How long will we keep the walls up? How long will we furiously defend against what we know deep down to be the truth of our lives?

Will we turn? Will we let the walls of our psyche fall with the walls of the Great Temple? Will we let in the truth we have been walling out all year long and let this truth help us to stop making the same mistakes again and again? Will we let this moment of consciousness help us break the unconscious momentum of our lives? Will we move from a state of siege to a state of openness, to a state of truthfulness, especially with ourselves?

What might we see as a result? What deep wellspring would suddenly become apparent to us? What pattern would we see ourselves repeating? What larger gesture would we see about to complete itself in our lives? What do we need to embrace?

The walls of our soul begin to crumble and the first glimmerings of transformation — of Teshuvah — begin to seep in. We turn and stop looking beyond ourselves. We stop defending ourselves. We stop blaming bad luck and circumstances and other people for our difficulties. We turn in and let the walls fall.

Our suffering, the unresolved element of our lives, is also from God. It is the instrument by which we are carried back to God, not something to be defended against, but rather to be embraced. And this embrace begins here on Tisha B'Av, seven weeks before Rosh Hashanah, so that by the Ten Days of Teshuvah, we are ready for transformation. We can enter the present moment of our lives and consciously alter that moment. We can end our exile.

We can step outside our walls and feel the full force of the great tidal pulls on our body and our soul; sun and moon, inhale and exhale, life and death, the walls building up and the walls crumbling down again.

—

CHAPTER FOUR

The Horn Blew

and I Began

to Wake Up

Elul

Suddenly you are awakened by a strange noise, a noise that fills the full field of your consciousness and then splits into several jagged strands, shattering that field, shaking you awake. The ram's horn, the shofar, the same instrument that will sound one hundred times on Rosh Hashanah, the same sound that filled the world when the Torah was spoken into being on Mount Sinai, is being blown to call you to wakefulness. You awake to confusion. Where are you? Who are you?

Then you remember. In exactly one month, one revolution of the moon, you will stand before God. What will God see on that day? What will you see? This encounter can carry you significantly closer to the truth of your life. Standing in the light of God, you can see a great deal more than you ordinarily might, but only to the degree that you are already awake, only in proportion to the time and energy you have devoted to preparing for this encounter.

So it is that the Mateh Moshe proclaimed, "Every person must prepare himself for thirty days beforehand with repentance and prayer and charity for the day when he will appear in judgment before God on Rosh Hashanah. Therefore let every person scrutinize their actions with a view to mending them. Let them exclude themselves for one hour every day and examine themselves," and Rabbi Chaim David Azulai declared, "During Elul [the month before Rosh Hashanah], one should devote less time to study and more time to fixed periods of introspection and self-evaluation," and the Kav Hayashar recorded that many men in his time observed silence between the advent of Elul and Rosh Hashanah to effect the purification of their souls.

The horn blows to usher in Elul, and it is blown every morning of the month of Elul as well, lest we forget and slip back, lest we surrender to the entropic pull of mindlessness. The Torah also stands ready to help keep us awake. As we move through the month of Elul, we also move through the Book of Deuteronomy, and each of the weekly Torah readings — Re'eh, Shoftim, Netzavim, Ki Tetze — whispers to us, "Wake up! Wake up!" Each of these readings offers a subtle rhyme to the process of awakening to which the month of Elul has called us.

Parshat Re'eh

"Look! I put before you this day a blessing and a curse." So begins Parshat Re'eh, the weekly Torah portion we read as the month of Elul begins. Look. Pay attention to your life. Every moment in it is profoundly mixed. Every moment contains a blessing and a

—

curse. Everything depends on our seeing our lives with clear eyes, seeing the potential blessing in each moment as well as the potential curse, choosing the former, forswearing the latter. Parshat Re'eh begins with a concretization of this spiritual reality, a ritual that renders this invisible reality visible.

As the Israelites crossed the Jordan River to enter the Promised Land, they staged a dramatic pageant. They wrote the word of God on twelve great stones and placed the stones on the peak of Mount Gerizim. Half of the nation of Israel stood on the slopes of Mount Gerizim and the other half stood on the slopes of Mount Ebal, across the valley. Standing in the valley between the two mountains, the priestly tribe, the Levites, faced Mount Gerizim and intoned a series of blessings, and all the people said Amen. Then the Levites faced the slopes of Mount Ebal and intoned a series of curses, and all the people said Amen again.

The message of this ritual was clear. The will of God is present every moment. Every moment contains the capacity for good and evil, life and death, a blessing and a curse, and everything depends on our choice. "Look. . . . I call Heaven and Earth to witness against you this day that I have set before you life and death, the blessing and the curse. Therefore choose life, so that you may live," Moses repeats in the ringing peroration to the Book of Deuteronomy.

We learn a number of things from this. We learn that this business of choosing good over evil, life over death, is precisely a matter of life and death. Our lives quite literally depend on it. And we learn that it is a matter of consciousness also. We have to come to see our life very clearly, clearly enough so that we can discern the will of God in it, so that we can tell the difference between the blessings and the curses, so that these things are arrayed before us as clearly as mountains, as we intone their names from the valley in between — that sliver of eternity on which we stand and that we call the present moment.

This is why we are advised to spend the month of Elul in the regular practice of introspection, self-examination, and silence. We no longer perform the great pageant of the blessings and the curses, Mount Gerizim and Mount Ebal. But this pageant was a ritual, and the inner process that this ritual was trying to express in visual form persists. Today we have our own ritualization of it: the Days of Awe, the High Holy Days, the time when it is made equally clear to us that everything depends upon our own moral and spiritual choices. And although we no longer have the two great mountains to help us see this choice in concrete form, we do have the month of Elul — a time to gaze upon the inner mountains, to devote serious attention to bringing our lives into focus; a time to clarify the distinction between the will of God and our own willfulness, to identify that in us which yearns for life and that which clings to death, that which seeks good and that which is fatally attracted to the perverse, to find out who we are and where we are going.

All the rabbis who comment on this period make it clear that we must do these things during the month of Elul. We must set aside time each day of Elul to look at ourselves, to engage in self-evaluation and self-judgment, to engage in *cheshbon-ha-nefesh*, literally a spiritual accounting. But we get very little in the way of practical advice as to how we might do this. So allow me to make some suggestions.

—

ॐ **Prayer** — The Hebrew word for prayer is *tefilah*. The infinitive form of this verb is *l'hitpalel* — to pray — a reflexive form denoting action that one performs on oneself. Many scholars believe that the root of this word comes from a Ugaritic verb for judgment, and that the reflexive verb *l'hitpalel* originally must have meant to judge oneself. This is not the usual way we think of prayer. Ordinarily we think we should pray to ask for things, or to bend God's will to our own. But it is no secret to those who pray regularly and with conviction that one of the deepest potentials of prayer is that it can be a way we come to know ourselves. This is true in at least two ways. First, when we pray, we stand before God — we invoke God's presence, we see ourselves through God's unblinking gaze. From this point of view, it becomes rather more difficult to engage in the kind of self-deception and highly selective interpretation of data we usually employ to make assessments of ourselves. God isn't as easy to deceive as we are. God has the annoying tendency of taking everything into account and not just the aspects of our experience that make us look good (or bad, if that's what we're up to). I have either meditated or prayed every day for the better part of the last thirty years. There have been a few occasions during this time when I've done something I knew to be wrong at the time that I did it. These times, for most of us, are rather rare. Most of the time, the negative, destructive things we do are done unconsciously. The remedy for this, of course, is simply to become more conscious, more aware. But what about those rare times when consciousness is not the problem? What about the times when we are perfectly conscious to begin with; when we say to ourselves, I know this is wrong, I know this is going to be hurtful and destructive both to myself and to others,

—

but damn it, I'm going to do it anyway? After performing such a deed, it is possible to go through much of one's life in denial or to construct elaborate justifications for why you did it. But it is impossible to employ such strategies while standing before God. Then, the naked truth of what we have done cannot be denied, and all our justifications crumble to dust. Standing before God, we see ourselves whether we want to or not.

It is also the case that there is something about the mechanics of prayer that causes us to know ourselves. Like all spiritual activities, Jewish communal prayer has a point of focus; in this case, the words of the prayer book. We try to concentrate on these words, but inevitably our mind wanders and we lose our focus. When we realize that this has happened, we bring our focus back to the words of the prayer book, and as we do, we catch a glimpse of what it is that has carried us away. This is an important thing to see. The thoughts that carry our attention away are never insignificant thoughts, and they never arise at random. We lose our focus precisely because these thoughts need our attention and we refuse to give it to them. This is why they keep sneaking up on our attention and stealing it away. This is how it is that we come to know ourselves as we settle deeply into the act of prayer. Most likely we are utterly unaware of all this. After all, it operates well below the level of consciousness. Nevertheless, sitting there with the prayer book in our lap, we begin to become aware of the things we have been trying to avoid; we begin to see things from which we have been averting our gaze; unconscious material begins to make its way toward the surface of our consciousness. So during the month of Elul, one of the times we can use to examine ourselves, to engage in self-assessment and self-judgment, is the time spent in

—

communal prayer. We can either devote more time to this activity, or if we already pray quite regularly, now we can do so with a more focused intention to have our praying become *tefilah* in the original sense — an act of self-judgment, an opportunity to see ourselves more clearly.

⚘ **Meditation** also presents us with this opportunity. Although much has been written in recent years about the various aspects of Jewish spiritual activity that resemble meditation, nowhere is this similarity more apparent than in the month of Elul, when we are bidden to set aside time each day to look inward, to take account of ourselves spiritually. Sitting each day at a specified time during the month of Elul, we may focus on our breath and our body, holding our body at the balance point between tension and relaxation, watching the breath as it enters and leaves the body just below the navel, letting the belly fill up with breath and then letting the breath go out. As we saturate these most fundamental aspects of our reality with awareness, we find that we are inhabiting ourselves in a deeper way than we usually do. And gradually this sense spreads to our heart and our mind and our soul, and we find that we are also inhabiting our feelings, our thoughts, and our spirit more deeply, that we are filling these things with more consciousness than we usually do, that we are feeling them more immediately, more concretely, more viscerally; in short, that we are coming to inhabit the present-tense reality of who we are, coming to see our real moral and spiritual position and what is required of us next.

Exactly the same phenomena we described in relation to prayer arise when we meditate — that moment of insight when we

—

bear witness to the thoughts that have carried our awareness away; that moment when we come to know precisely what these thoughts are, precisely what it is that we aren't looking at and so keeps sneaking up on us and grabbing our attention. In fact, it is just this process that the physiologist Herbert Benson identifies as the fundamental gesture of meditation, the gesture he calls the Relaxation Response. According to Benson, all the brain wave changes and psychospiritual effects we have come to associate with meditation are set off precisely at the moment when we come to realize that our mind has been carried away from the object of our concentration and we resolve to gently bring it back. When we were speaking of prayer, it was the words of the prayer book that we were trying to focus on. Here in meditation, it might be the breath and it might be the body, it might be a mantra and it might be a visualization, but in all these cases, the result is the same: we come to see ourselves more clearly. We come to see the things we either will not or cannot see.

And meditation helps us see something else as well; it helps us see that we are something larger than ourselves. This is an essential aspect of Rosh Hashanah — seeing ourselves as not just a discrete ego, but as part of a great flow of being. The very first thing the Talmud has to say about Rosh Hashanah is this:

On Rosh Hashanah, all the inhabitants of the earth stand before God, as it says in the Thirty-third Psalm, "[God] fashions their hearts as one, and discerns all their actions together."

When we sit in meditation with other people, breathing the same air, hearing the same sounds, thinking thoughts in the same rhythms and patterns, we experience our connection to each other in a very immediate way. This connection is not merely an idea; it is our heartfelt, visceral reality. This is an important part of the process of seeing ourselves. Meditation helps us inhabit ourselves more deeply, and it constantly throws us up against the very things about ourselves we are trying not to see. But it carries the process of insight one step further; it helps us to see that we are not merely our individual selves, but part of something much more vast as well.

⚅ **Focus on one thing** — It may not be realistic to expect a significant number of people to suddenly begin showing up at prayer minyans or meditation groups during the month of Elul — some of us are simply not made to engage in these activities; not in Elul, not ever. Many will never get over finding the daily prayer service tedious and opaque. Many others will always either be frightened to death or bored to tears by the prospect of meditation and the blank wall of self it keeps throwing us up against so relentlessly. So I am pleased to inform you that it is perfectly possible to fulfill the ancient imperative to begin becoming more self-aware during this time without doing these things. Let me recommend a simpler method, and you won't even have to set aside a special time to practice this; you have set aside the time already. Just choose one simple and fundamental aspect of your life and commit yourself to being totally conscious and honest about it for the thirty days of Elul. "A world in a grain of sand," as the poet William Blake reminded us. Everything we do is an expression of the entire truth of our lives. It doesn't really make any difference what it is that we choose to focus on, but it ought to be something

—

pretty basic, something like eating or sex or money, if for no other reason than that these concerns are likely to arise quite frequently in our lives and to give us a lot of grist for the mill.

Parshat Re'eh has some interesting things to say about eating, for example, that might be helpful in this regard. After the ancient Israelites offered a sacrifice, they were bidden to eat it, but "only all that your soul desires." This is a strange phrase, is it not? "Only all that your soul desires." What could it mean? "All that your soul desires" seems to suggest an unlimited condition. What then is the force of the limiting "only" in this sentence? I think what the Torah is saying here is that we should only eat until we are satiated. "You shall eat and you shall reach the point of satiety and then you shall bless the Lord your God." This familiar imperative is also found in Parshat Re'eh, and it expresses the same thing. We should eat to the point of satiety, but not beyond that point. We should eat only what our soul desires, only what our body requires, and not what our unconscious desires bid us to eat.

I think it's a very rare thing that we eat out of hunger these days, and it is even rarer that we stop eating when our hunger is slaked. At a rabbinical retreat once, a man gave me a stress-measuring device called a biodot. The biodot was a tiny piece of paper treated with a chemical that responded to changes in temperature by changing color. The idea was that when we were under stress our fight-or-flight instinct rushed all the blood to the extremities of the body, where it would be needed. All this blood rushing to our hands raised the temperature there, so when we were under stress, the biodot registered this change in temperature by turning black. In happier, more relaxed states, the blood settled back into the heart and the inner organs, leaving the hands much cooler. At such

—

times the biodot turned green, and then finally, when we were in the deepest state of relaxation, a radiant, cerulean blue.

Back from the retreat, I watched the biodot changing color as I went about my daily life for several weeks. I noticed, for example, that as soon as I walked into my synagogue, the dot turned a livid, menacing black. It made no difference what I did there. I could pray, I could meditate for hours, but just being in the building threw me into a deep state of stress. Conversely there were activities that were just as dependable for producing the bright blue color that indicated a state of relaxation so deep it bordered on bliss. Chief among these was eating. Whenever I ate, the biodot turned its most radiant blue. Clearly eating was an activity with profound emotional and spiritual reverberations, and just as clearly it was an activity that resided at the opposite end of the emotional spectrum from stress. Suddenly it seemed pretty obvious why eating often becomes something other than the simple act of satisfying our physical hunger. Eating is a fast palliative for the stress that overwhelms us, a surrogate for the emotional and spiritual nourishment we need and never receive, a way of feeling our physicality in a world that all too rarely permits us to do so. In short, the act of eating is a gateway to some of our deepest feelings. This is why, if we just make a simple resolve to only eat in truth during the month of Elul — to eat only when we are truly hungry, "only all that your soul desires" — I think we'll be amazed how much of the truth of our lives we'll dredge up, what a complex of repressed feeling and dysfunction this simple focus will bring floating up to the forefront of our consciousness.

The same thing would happen if we made a similar resolve regarding sexual activity, which is if anything even more

—

emotionally charged. A congregant came to me recently to tell me of his experience in doing precisely this. One day he had realized that he had never been honest about the most intimate aspects of his marital relationship. Physically and emotionally, he had been hiding who he really was, pretending to be always eager for sex when the truth was that sometimes he was and sometimes he wasn't, ignoring the waves of ambiguity he often felt in the midst of sex for fear of hurting his wife, fending off the deepest sort of intimacy for fear of revealing himself to another human being. Suddenly conscious of all this, he had resolved to live this part of his life as truthfully as he possibly could, to stop pretending, to stop ignoring, to stop fending off, and this single resolve had begun to transform not only his marriage, but the rest of his life as well. Sometimes his new candor did in fact hurt his wife's feelings, but they always managed to get over it — to talk it out — and they felt so much closer now that they couldn't imagine how they had managed to live at such a distance from each other before. And this man now found himself unwilling to hide himself at work either, and this had changed his entire relationship to his job. Realizing that he could really be himself at work had removed the single greatest source of stress there, and he now found himself enjoying his work in a way he never had before.

Money, like food and sex, can be another fruitful object of mindful focus. I recently enrolled in a computerized banking service. Every day the computer shows me a complete breakdown of every financial transaction I make, every penny I spend. I find that I am no longer able to entertain fantasies about how I spend money. The computer rubs my nose in the truth every day. Every day, I have to face the reality of my neurotic compulsions and dependencies.

—

Every day, I have to look at a very precise record of what is really important to me, what my priorities really are — a very different matter, in most cases, from what I imagine them to be.

The truth of our lives is reflected in everything we do, and if we focus on even one small part of our lives, it brings up the entire truth of it.

So we can pray, we can meditate, and we can set aside a moment every day for reflection. Or we can simply choose one thing in our life and live that one small aspect in truth, and then watch in amazement as the larger truth of our life begins to emerge. The truth is, every moment of our life carries with it the possibility of a great blessing and a great curse, a blessing if we live in truth, a curse if we do not.

This is the time of year we are bidden to know the truth. In fact, we are commanded to do so. *Re'eh* — look, pay attention — for I have put before you a great blessing and a considerable curse, right there in the moment before you. All that's required of you is to see what's in front of your face and to choose the blessing in it.

PARSHAT SHOFTIM

I once went for a hike with my son, Stephen, who is an entomologist, in a nature preserve on Martha's Vineyard. A storm came up and we had to take refuge in a little shack with a big picture window. I sat looking out the window in the rain at the birds and other flora and fauna of Martha's Vineyard, none of which was all that compelling. My son, on the other hand, was having a much more interesting time. He was looking, not *through* the window at what was outside, but rather *at* the window itself. The window, he soon pointed out to me, was a very active world in and of itself, a nature preserve for insect life, as it were. And in fact, when I gave my full attention to the window instead of just looking through it, it turned out to be a veritable wonderland, full of gossamer membranes, spherical silver eggs, and metallic silver flies like Art Deco flying machines. It was clear this window wasn't just something through which to view the world; it was a world in itself, a place with a life of its own.

Parshat Shoftim, which we read during the first or second week of the month of Elul, begins with what seems like a simple prescription for the establishment of a judicial system. "Judges and officers you shall appoint for yourselves in all your gates." But the great Hasidic Torah commentary, the Iturey Torah, read this passage as an imperative of a very different sort — an imperative for a kind of inner mindfulness. According to the Iturey Torah, there are seven gates — seven windows — to the soul: the two eyes, the two ears, the two nostrils, and the mouth. Everything that passes into our consciousness must enter through one of these gates. So at the deepest level, the passage cited above has nothing to do with establishment of a system of judges and courts, but deals rather with being mindful of the process of consciousness itself.

The essential act of the High Holiday season is Teshuvah, a turning toward mindfulness, and an important step in this process is a kind of turning in to examine our perceptive mechanisms, the way we see the world. It is a shifting of our gaze from the world itself to the window through which we see it, because that window, the screen of our consciousness, is not just a blank, transparent medium. Rather it is a world unto itself, a world teeming with

—

77

life, and that life affects what we see. And because that life makes us see the world differently, the first step in Teshuvah is to look at the window itself. When the shofar blows on the first day of Elul and every morning thereafter, it reminds us to turn our gaze inward, and to place judgment at the gates of our consciousness, to shift our focus from the outside world to the considerable activity taking place in the window through which we view it.

There are several very powerful suggestions later on in Parshat Shoftim as to precisely what it is we should be looking for during the month of Elul as we turn toward the gates of the soul in preparation for Teshuvah. These suggestions come, oddly enough, in the laws of war that are enunciated toward the end of the *parshah*. Before Israel goes off to war, the Torah tells us, the officers of the army must address the people and tell them the following:

> Who is the man who has built a new house but has not yet inhabited it? Let him go and return to his house, lest he die in the war and another man inhabit his house.
>
> Who is the man who has planted a vineyard and has not yet harvested it? Let him go and return to his house, lest he die in the war and another man harvest it.
>
> Who is the man who has been betrothed to a woman but has yet not taken her to wife? Let him go and return to his house, lest he die in the war and another man take her.

The idea of all this seems to be that if we leave something incomplete, we fall into the state of mind the rabbis called *trafe da'at* — a torn mind — a mind pulled in various directions. A person in such a state of mind would be of little use in an army. He would be unable to focus on the task at hand and might even present a danger to his fellow soldiers. During a brief stint as a prison chaplain, I once spoke to a gang member who described what it was like to go to war with his fellow gang members. He spoke glowingly of the sense of total trust you had to have in the person in front of you and the person behind you. Your very life hung on their doing what they were supposed to do. But if they were in a state of *trafe da'at* — if there was unfinished business pulling their awareness away from the present moment — they wouldn't be trustworthy. In fact they would pose a real threat to your survival.

We see this very clearly around death. The threefold repetition of the phrase "lest he die" is not insignificant. In my work as a hospice chaplain, I often witnessed the irresistible urge people have to tie up loose ends as death approaches — to leave their checkbook balanced, to make their funeral arrangements, to finally confess to something that has been on their conscience, to make reconciliation with a friend or a loved one. The urge to complete unfinished business, to tie up loose ends, is one of the strongest forces in nature, and God help anyone who stands in its way. In my experience, this is the single most common source of family conflict around death. The person who is dying asks his family to help him balance his checkbook, or purchase a plot in a cemetery, but the members of his family, still alive, healthy, and very much caught up in the full-time occupation of denying death, don't want to listen. "What are you talking about?" they tell him. "You're not going to die," a response that provokes unbearable frustration and alienation in the dying, who desperately need to do these

—

things. When this need is ignored, they feel more than ever that they are facing death alone.

But like everything else about death, this urge is only an intensification of what happens throughout life. Death is merely a time when what is usually unconscious and invisible becomes conscious and visible. So while we are conducting spiritual inventory during Elul, we might begin by asking ourselves, What are the loose ends in my life? How is my mind torn? Where are the places my mind keeps wanting to go? What is the unfinished business in my life? What have I left undone? When we look out at the world through a torn mind, our experience of the world is torn.

In some cases we might decide that it's just time to let go — to recognize that we are distracted by something that will never be completed — and in some cases, we might decide that the only cure is in fact completion; that there's nothing for it but to tie up that loose end, no way to keep our energy and focus from constantly draining away from the present-tense reality of our actual experience except to finish that which remains unfinished.

Life is impossibly complex. We are all like jugglers with too many balls in the air by far. Taking a clear look at our lives, we might simply decide that we can't possibly complete all the unfinished business we've set in motion. Finally coming home at nine or ten at night, from a day at work that began at six A.M., our mind torn to shreds by the thought of all the phone calls we never had time to return and the tasks we couldn't complete, we might sense, in a moment of quiet, how much pain all of this has left us in.

So when we are taking inventory, one of the things we might decide is that we have to simplify our lives. We have to do fewer things. We have to go to our bosses, or we have to tell ourselves,

—

Look, there is just too much on my plate. I'm *trafe da'at* — I'm unfocused; I'm torn. The energy of that undedicated house, that unharvested vineyard, that unconsummated marriage — all that energy is tearing my mind, pulling my focus in a hundred directions and leaving me not much good for anything.

And worst of all, it is causing me to look out at the world through a shattered window. Perhaps that's why the world seems so torn to me. I think this might be a very important thing to look at during Elul, while we are examining the glass in front of our face, the window to the soul.

But there was another instruction officers were required to give their troops toward the end of Parshat Shoftim, and this instruction also points us to something we might be looking at during this month of Elul as we turn toward the gates of the soul in preparation for Teshuvah. "Who is the man who is fearful and faint-hearted? Let him go and return to his house, lest his brother's heart melt as his heart has." The assumption beneath this admonition is staggering in both its scope and its simplicity: we all share the same heart. We penetrate each other far more than we are ordinarily aware. Ordinarily we are taken in by the materialist myth of discrete being. We look like we are separate bodies. We look like we are discrete from one another. Physically we can see where one of us begins and another of us ends, but emotionally, spiritually, it simply isn't this way. Our feelings and our spiritual impulses flow freely beyond the boundaries of the self, and this is something that each of us knows intuitively for a certainty.

We know, for example, that when we go to visit a friend and they are depressed and we talk to them for a while, when we leave them, they will feel better but we will feel worse. Or if we're at a football game, we will feel the excitement of the crowd in our own person, passing through us, penetrating our discrete physical boundaries, ignoring these boundaries completely.

We know that emotions are contagious. We know they do not honor the boundaries of self, and even seem to mock them. We all have the same heart. So if someone is afraid, the Torah tells us, we had better send him home from battle before the fear spreads from his heart to ours. The fear is more real than the self.

But this emotional contagion is not limited to fear. Fear is only one example of what ripples soul to soul and heart to heart. Love also does this. So does happiness. So does suffering.

Parshat Netzavim, another of the Torah portions we read during the month of Elul, contains some very good advice about how to accomplish this business of spiritual accounting.

Where is this thing called Teshuvah located? the Torah asks. Well, it isn't in heaven, so please don't say, I can't do this thing because I don't know how to get to heaven. And it isn't across the sea, so please don't say, I can't do this thing because I don't have a steamship ticket. "Rather it is exceedingly near to you, in your mouth and in your heart, so you can do it." Don't look off in the distance, and don't look outside yourself either, the Torah is telling us, look at your own heart. Don't look out the window; look at the window itself.

What is the pain that is pressing on your heart right this moment? That's what you need to make Teshuvah about. You need to make Teshuvah about your fractured mind and your fearful heart.

What is occluding the deep connection between you and your fellow human beings? That is also right there over your heart, and that also needs to be looked at. One of the things that most often impedes this connection is our fear of one another's pain. We have already established that we all have one heart. Deep down, we know this very well. But what we are usually not aware of is how much we feel other people's pain and how much energy we waste trying to defend ourselves against it.

Recently I was counseling two close friends. They were having a fight and I was pretty well caught in the middle of it. One of these people was suffering terribly from loneliness, and because of this he had made impossible demands on his friend. The second fellow was overburdened by work and overstressed by family problems to begin with and so became very angry at his friend for the demands he was making. And there I was in the middle, feeling the first guy's loneliness intensely and the second guy's stress and frustration just as strongly. But instead of feeling empathy for them, I found that I was getting angry at both of them. Suddenly I felt very critical feelings toward them. Why? Because I felt I was responsible for them and their pain. I felt I had to do something about it, and because I knew there was nothing I could do, because I knew I was powerless to make their pain go away, I was doing the next best thing. I was trying to keep it at arm's length, to defend myself against it. Of course, that was impossible. We can't help feeling each other's pain. We all share the same heart. If someone else is suffering, there's no way we can shut it out. It spreads heart to heart and soul to soul, a movement that is absolutely irresistible, like the waters of a flood.

And I started to wonder, How many people am I angry at? How many people do I harbor ungenerous feelings toward, simply because I am privy to their suffering and frightened by it, and so need to keep it at bay with anger and criticism?

—

But the problem is never the suffering. The problem is our feeling that we have to do something about it. I often visit people in hospitals, and over the years I've gotten into the habit of doing a special meditation at the threshold of each hospital room. I stand in the threshold breathing deeply until I can feel the fear that always follows me into these rooms. It is the fear of not being able to do anything to help the person who is ill. What, after all, can I do? Can I make their illness go away? If they are dying, can I forestall their death? Perhaps I can comfort them, but what if I say the wrong thing and make things even worse? So I stand in the doorway until I feel this fear come up, as it always does, until it has filled me completely, and then I remind myself that I am not going into that room to *do* anything for the person who is ill. Rather, I am going there to *be* with them, to listen to them, to offer them the only gift that makes any difference at all in this transaction, the gift of my presence.

And when this meditation works and I really am able to simply be with them and let their feelings flow naturally from their heart to mine, it is almost always a beautiful experience, a rich experience for me, whatever effect it may have on them, and it's quite clear that there is nothing to fear from their suffering when it flows from their heart to my heart. Suffering is just suffering, a feeling that only wants release from the imprisonment of the self — a spiritual impulse that often ennobles, and that like any feeling, carries its own considerable burden of beauty with it.

And this is even true of fear, and of anger, and of every other feeling that spreads heart to heart until it has filled the world. It is true of love, and it is true of compassion.

—

So even if we're not going off to war, these ancient laws of war are still extremely useful, especially during the month of Elul, as we stand watch at the gate of our soul, as we turn our attention from what is outside the window to the window itself.

What unfinished business, what unnecessary complexity is making us *trafe da'at*, is tearing our focus away from the present-tense reality of our experience, from the present moment, the only place where we can really have our lives?

And what shadow of fear or anger — what imagined impotence — is keeping us from a deep emotional and spiritual connection to the people around us?

Is the world really torn and dark, or does it just appear that way to us because we are taking it in through a torn mind and a hardened heart?

Judges you shall put in all your gates. This is how Teshuvah begins. When Elul comes around again, watch the window. Keep a mindful eye on the gates of the soul.

Parshat Ki Tetze

Oddly enough, Parshat Ki Tetze, which we read during the third week of Elul, also derives a lesson in the kind of mindfulness we are trying to cultivate during this month from the laws of war. Images of war abound during Elul. On the first day of Elul we begin to add the Twenty-seventh Psalm to our morning and evening prayers. "Though armies are arrayed against me, I will have no fear. Though war threatens, I will remain steadfast in my faith," reads the Twenty-seventh Psalm. It is as if the tradition is trying to tell us, "This business of becoming aware of ourselves is a matter of life and death. This business of finding out who we really are needs to be approached with the focus and energy of a military campaign."

In any case, whereas Parshat Shoftim derives its lessons about mindful awareness from the moment just before battle, Ki Tetze focuses on the moment just afterward.

When you have been victorious in battle, this *parshah* begins, and you are carrying away your captives,

> and you see among the captives a beautiful woman with a good figure and you feel desire for her and you want to take her to yourself to be your wife, first, you must bring her into your house and have her shave her head, and cut off her fingernails, and remove the dress she was wearing when you captured her. She must remain in your house weeping for her father and her mother for a full month, and after that you may come to her and be her husband.

This passage deals with a rather ugly human impulse that is as ancient as the hills and as current as the day before yesterday. Men, victorious in war, raging testosterone unleashed by battle and now utterly unrestrained, grab and rape the first women they see on the streets of the cities they have just vanquished. Ancient art and literature and yesterday's newspapers are full of this disturbing human tendency — Greek and Shakespearean tragedy, *The Rape of the Sabine Women*, the Serbo-Croatian wars. Desire run amok has always been and continues to be one of the most troublesome of human impulses. Nor are the implements for arousing desire any less universal or current. Elul always falls in the late summer, and I do weddings almost every Sunday then. Standing under the chuppah with bride and groom on the week we read Parshat Ki Tetze, I am often reminded that carefully done fingernails, well-coifed hair, and alluring dresses are still frequently employed to arouse a passion in a man sufficient to get him under the wedding canopy.

The Torah is not really concerned with the specific case of the woman captured in battle. I think it has a larger principle in mind in all this. It seems to be suggesting a method for dealing with the tyranny of passion and desire in our lives in general. The raging lust of the victorious soldier is merely one instance, one example, of that desire for which we humans throw away our lives, the living death we bring upon ourselves. The poet John Keats maps out this territory very well in his poem "La Belle Dame Sans Merci."

"She took me to her elfin grot
    And there she wept and sighed full sore;
And there I shut her wild wild eyes
    With kisses four.

"And there she lulled me asleep,
    And there I dreamed, Ah! Woe betide!
The latest dream I ever dreamed
    On the cold hill's side.

—

"I saw pale kings and princes too,
　Pale warriors, death-pale were they all;
They cried, 'La Belle Dame sans Merci
　Hath thee in thrall!'

"I saw their starved lips in the gloam
　With horrid warning gaped wide,
And I awoke and found me here
　On the cold hill's side.

"And this is why I sojourn here
　Alone and palely loitering,
Though the sedge is withered from the lake
　And no birds sing."

The kind of impulse Keats describes arises in our lives in many forms. It shows itself in the impulse that might seduce us into a ruinous midlife affair, or that might cause us to sacrifice our families for ambition, or to give up our heart's work for the pursuit of material excess, or to give up our integrity for fame and fortune, or God for the pursuit of pleasure.

Given how pernicious and pervasive such impulses are, how much damage they could do to us, we might find ourselves asking this: Why doesn't the Torah just do away with them altogether? Why doesn't the Torah just tell us not to take the woman captive in the first place?

I think there might be several ways of answering this question. First off, it would have been unrealistic for the Torah to have done so, and the Torah is, above all, an extremely realistic work.

—

The Torah never permits too much distance between the values it proposes and the way people actually behave, because it recognizes that to do so would break the connection between our lives and the Torah, between our lives and the will of God. So the Torah can't afford to do too much violence to the way we are, and this lustful impulse, unfortunately, has been repeated throughout human history.

But trying to efface the impulse altogether might not only have been unrealistic, it might have been undesirable. Like everything we have been given in this life, this impulse might also have its place, its use. This impulse in fact might be part and parcel of the process of human creativity. This, at least, is the suggestion of a story that is told in the Talmud, in Masecet Yoma. The Children of Israel, it seems, once prayed to God that the impulse that tempted them into sexual misconduct be handed over to them as a captive. After they fasted for three days and nights, this tempter was in fact handed over to them. The prophet warned them that if they killed it, they would bring the world down with it, so they imprisoned it for three days instead. But there wasn't a fresh egg to be found in the entire land of Israel for those three days. Finally they just put out its eyes and let it loose again.

The Talmud seems to be saying that this business of desire is the basis of our creativity, our productivity. Our desire for the apple in the Garden of Eden got us kicked out of Eden, but it also propelled us into history, and if we try to squelch it, or bury it, we might stop being productive. History might grind to a halt.

Since we can't and probably shouldn't repress our desires, and since it is so often a calamity when we follow them, what should we do?

—

The passage from Parshat Ki Tetze points us to an answer. First of all, we watch our desires arise. The soldier at the beginning of Parshat Ki Tetze has to live with his desire, to watch it as it evolves without acting on it, for a full month. And the second thing we can learn from him is that once we have our desires firmly in view, we can then strip them of their exotic dress. We can make them cut off their fingernails and their hair, we can make them take off that revealing frock they were wearing when we first saw them. In other words, we can see them for what they really are.

In his autobiography of his early teenage years, *The Basketball Diaries*, the poet Jim Carroll writes about a moment when he saw his own displaced passion stripped of its exotic disguise. Already a notorious womanizer, Carroll found himself on a long, slow elevator one day with a beautiful woman for whom he felt an immediate sexual longing. He wanted to make a move right away, but there were other people on the elevator, so acting on this longing was not an option. But as the elevator made its seemingly endless ascent, he began to realize that in truth, he had no desire to make love to this woman at all. That impulse he was feeling was a dozen other things. It was the need to have his very weak ego affirmed by still another conquest. It was the need to cover up the bottomless pit of emptiness he felt at the core of his being with a rush of strong sensation. With this impulse now stripped bare of its exotic dress, Carroll understood not only that he didn't have to act on it, but that, moreover, he didn't even want to.

Why do we run after ambition? Why do we need fame and fortune? Why do we need to have a sexual conquest? If we try to push these desires down, they'll only come up somewhere else. If we kill them off altogether, we may be doing violence to ourselves; we may be killing off the basis of our real creativity.

Better to simply strip these desires of their romance and then watch them for a month before acting on them, before taking them to yourself. And what better time to do this than the month of Elul, the month we are supposed to devote to the regular cultivation of self-awareness, the month in which we begin the process of Teshuvah by shifting our gaze from the world outside to the consciousness through which we view that world. Certainly desire is a significant component of that consciousness, perhaps the most significant component.

So this is something else we can do during the month of Elul. We can devote a bit of time each day to locating our own particular *belle dame sans merci,* to identifying whatever desire has distorted our lives, the beautiful delusion for which we've thrown everything away, or for which we stand ready to do so, in any case.

And when we've located it, all we have to do is look at it. We don't have to kill it, and we certainly don't have to act on it either. We can just let it arise in the fullness of its being, unromantically stripped down to the naked impulse that it is, without the finery of romance, without hair, nails, or dress, just the bare impulse itself.

We can watch this impulse as it arises for the entire month of Elul, and if after a month it still seems to be something that we want, something that continues to arouse strong feeling in us, then we've learned something useful about ourselves.

But if this desire stripped of its romantic trappings simply fades away, then we've learned something even more useful. We've learned that there is more to heaven and earth than those things

—

on the surface of the world that provoke desire in our hearts. We've learned that if we always act on our desires, on those un-mitigated impulses that constantly rise up in our hearts and our minds, then we are doomed to a living death, doomed to be always palely loitering after a lock of hair, and a bit of nail and cloth, the ghostly phantoms of desire.

"Wait on God. Be strong and courageous of heart and wait on God."

This is the very good advice of that same Twenty-seventh Psalm we recite twice each day during the month of Elul. Better to wait on God. Better to just watch our impulses arise and wait for truth, wait for something deeper. Better to be strong and brave of heart than to surrender our lives to the empty stuff of desire, and to spend the rest of our lives palely loitering on a cold hillside where no birds sing.

CHAPTER FIVE

THIS IS REAL
AND YOU ARE
COMPLETELY UNPREPARED

SELICHOT

A MINDFUL AWARENESS OF OUR CIRCUMSTANCES often makes things seem worse and not better. This is an illusion, of course, but it doesn't feel like one, especially when we are in the first throes of discovery. Suddenly aware of problems we never knew we had, we may genuinely feel that we are much worse off than we thought we were; we may feel a sense of urgency, even of desperation, about our plight. This urgent, desperate sense is the emotional basis of Selichot, the week of urgent, desperate prayer that commences approximately three weeks into the process of daily contemplation we began with the blowing of the shofar on the first day of Elul.

—

Traditionally, Selichot begins with a midnight prayer service on the Saturday night before Rosh Hashanah (or on the previous Saturday night, if there are fewer than four days between that Saturday and Rosh Hashanah) and continues with special prayers of supplication recited by the pious at dawn each day of the following week. But even if we are not so pious, even if we don't attend the Selichot service on Saturday night that serves as a kind of grand overture to the High Holiday season, we may still feel a sense of urgency, a sense of desperation as Rosh Hashanah approaches. This is particularly true if we have been paying attention to the larger process; if we began on Tisha B'Av by allowing ourselves to be reminded of the ways we have become alienated from ourselves and from God; if we heard the shofar blow on the first day of Elul and began a month of contemplation and taking account of our souls. After all, in less than one week we will stand before God. If we are tuned in to this reality, we can't help but feel urgent and desperate now.

The ritual of Selichot is first mentioned in an obscure compilation of medieval Midrash, the Tanna D'Veit Eliyuahu Zuta.

David knew that the Temple would be destroyed in the future and the sacrificial cult would be nullified, and David was troubled thinking, how will Israel make atonement then? So God said to David, when troubles come upon Israel, let them

1. stand before me together as a single unit
2. and make confession before me
3. and say the selichot (forgiveness) service before me and I will answer them.

—

But how did God reveal these services to Israel? God came down from the heavenly mist like a sheliach tzibur (a cantor) wrapped in a tallit, and revealed to Moses the order of the service of forgiveness.

There are many things about this rabbinic legend that strike a deep chord, but the first arresting image is the one of all of Israel standing before God *ba'agudat achat* — as a single spiritual unit. I always feel that sense acutely during the High Holiday season, and especially on the first night of Rosh Hashanah, when we gather in great numbers for the first time. I'll never forget my first year in San Francisco, when I saw this for the first time. I had come from my tiny synagogue in Monroe, New York; there we packed a few hundred people into our little building and were quite impressed with ourselves for it. But in San Francisco, I looked out at what seemed like an endless sea of humanity — more people than I had ever spoken in front of before — and I felt a terror come over me.

A man who had been to Monroe as part of the search process was sitting beside me chortling softly. He knew exactly what I was feeling. But I don't think he realized how deep that moment was — that it was a kind of karmic replication of one of the most traumatic moments in my family's history.

My mother grew up in the Depression in a succession of tenements and basement flats in Coney Island, New York. Her father was a mild-mannered floor scraper by day, but on evenings and weekends, he ran the most important synagogue choir in New York. He loved music intensely. It threw him into an ecstasy. Whether it was a classic piece of *hazanut* (cantorial music), or Mozart, or a piece of bubble gum pop music on the radio, my

—

zadie savored it all. He cherished it. He closed his eyes as he sang or listened to it, and he went somewhere else altogether. I remember standing next to him on the altar during the High Holidays and looking up at his face and wondering where in God's name he was, because he certainly wasn't here.

Zadie was an autodidact. He had taught himself to play the piano and to read music. When he was engaged in that music, he was elsewhere — passionately and yearningly elsewhere. And he was determined to pass this great passion for music on to my mother, his eldest child, and to make sure that she could go much farther with it than he had been able to. As soon as my mother was old enough to sit up straight at the piano, he and she began to make the long trek to the Henry Street Settlement on the Lower East Side of Manhattan, so that she could begin piano lessons there.

The Henry Street Settlement was one of those wonderful agencies FDR established during the Depression to make sure that American artists, writers, and musicians didn't wither away and die during the hard economic times. At Henry Street, world-class musicians offered free music lessons to the poor kids of New York. It was a pure meritocracy. No one paid a dime, but they only took kids who had considerable talent and an even more pronounced willingness to work very hard. My mother had both, and by the time she was a teenager, the Henry Street teachers had managed to turn her into something of a prodigy. She played piano like an angel, and she continued to practice like a demon. She gave concerts all over the city to adoring, enthusiastic crowds, and then one day, when she was sixteen years old, she found herself seated at the grand piano on the stage of Carnegie Hall, the mecca of concert pianists. She was playing in the finals of the great citywide competition held at Carnegie Hall every year in those days. Brilliant pianists, prodigies from all over the city, played off against each other for a period of months, until the field was narrowed down to just two. A great deal was at stake. The winner would receive a full scholarship to the Juilliard School and be sent on a nationwide concert tour.

My mother had made mincemeat of all opposition, and now came the big moment she had been preparing for all her life. In the months leading up to this concert, she practiced the piece she would play every day with an urgent intensity. But none of that work had even begun to prepare her for the reality of this moment. She walked out onto the Carnegie stage and saw a great sea of faces — more human beings than she had ever seen in one place before, a multitude that dwarfed the audiences at the music parlors and high school auditoriums where she was used to playing. And when my mother reached the piano bench and sat down, she suddenly realized that all her preparations were inadequate for the intense reality of this actual moment, and she completely appled. She choked. She froze. She forgot what piece she was supposed to play. I'm not sure she was even conscious that she was supposed to be playing a piece at all. She just sat there on the stage of Carnegie Hall, frozen in terror, for a long, long time.

A quiet whisper began to come up from the great crowd, then a distinctly audible buzz. What was going on? How long was this chubby girl going to sit there doing nothing? Eventually — after a very, very long time — her teacher from Henry Street came out from backstage and sat down beside her and began to play the piece my mother had prepared, something by Mozart, I believe, or possibly Chopin. And after a very few bars, my mother began to come to her senses and to play along with him, and then finally he stopped and she made it through the rest of the piece on her own. She played haltingly and with many mistakes — her concentration was shot, of course, so she didn't play well — but she did make it through to the end, and then she ran off the stage to a smattering of polite, pitying applause. That was the end of her career as a concert pianist.

I fared better in San Francisco that night. I stared the crowd down and gave my speech. My mother was redeemed.

❦

Every year before the Days of Awe, the Ba'al Shem Tov, the founder of Hasidic Judaism, held a competition to see who would blow the shofar for him on Rosh Hashanah. Now if you wanted to blow the shofar for the Ba'al Shem Tov, not only did you have to blow the shofar like a virtuoso, but you also had to learn an elaborate system of *kavanot* — secret prayers that were said just before you blew the shofar to direct the shofar blasts and to see that they had the proper effect in the supernal realms. All the prospective shofar blowers practiced these kavanot for months. They were difficult and complex. There was one fellow who wanted to blow the shofar for the Ba'al Shem Tov so badly that he had been practicing these kavanot for years. But when his time came to audition before the Ba'al Shem, he realized that nothing he had done had prepared him adequately for the experience of standing before this great and holy man, and he appled. He choked. His mind froze completely. He couldn't remember one of the kavanot he had practiced for all those years. He couldn't

—

even remember what he was supposed to be doing at all. He just stood before the Ba'al Shem in utter silence, and then, when he realized how egregiously — how utterly — he had failed this great test, his heart just broke in two and he began to weep, sobbing loudly, his shoulders heaving and his whole body wracking as he wept.

All right, you're hired, the Ba'al Shem said.

But I don't understand, the man said. I failed the test completely. I couldn't even remember one *kavanah*.

So the Ba'al Shem explained with the following parable: In the palace of the King, there are many secret chambers, and there are secret keys for each chamber, but one key unlocks them all, and that key is the ax. The King is the Lord of the Universe, the Ba'al Shem explained. The palace is the House of God. The secret chambers are the *sefirot*, the ascending spiritual realms that bring us closer and closer to God when we perform commandments such as blowing the shofar with the proper intention, and the secret keys are the kavanot. And the ax — the key that opens every chamber and brings us directly into the presence of the King, wherever he may be — the ax is the broken heart, for as it says in the Psalms, "God is close to the brokenhearted."

Please imagine this: You are out for a social evening with those very close to you, family or close friends or both. The evening begins with a wonderful dinner, and then, out of some vague sense — or perhaps a very strong sense — of family tradition and obligation, you all go off after dinner to participate in a basically empty religious ritual. Or perhaps you are by yourself, but you attend this empty ritual because you have very pleasant associations of having done so with your family and friends back in Cleveland or Detroit or New Jersey. Or perhaps it is not so empty for you. Perhaps you feel a great deal at this service, but you're really not sure if it's you or the service; if it's the ritual itself or that peculiar pain you have been feeling in your heart lately. Or perhaps you feel very little, but every year you harbor the hope that you will feel something this time, even though you never really do, and you always feel a little disappointed about this. But you don't really mind attending this ritual. After all, it's tradition, and even though you are sleepy from all the food, the music is lovely and the officiant is sometimes mildly amusing when he speaks. But basically you go not because you antici-pate that anything significant will happen, but rather because this is what the family does every year at this time. Or this is what you used to do with them. This is what you have always done, so you will do it this year too.

But this time as you enter the sanctuary, everything feels differ-ent. So you look more closely. There are three immense books at the head of the sanctuary. A presence can be felt in the room so palpably you can almost see it; it hovers over the table like a colloid suspension, a smoky mist. Now you hear a deep, disembodied voice calling out names, and every time a name is called, it is written in one of the books. There is no hand, there is no quill; the pages of the book simply rustle and then quiver, and when the rustling stops, the name is already written. It is written in the Book of Life, while sighs of relief go up all around the room; or it is written in the Book of Death, while a cold silence grips the sanctuary, amid much shuddering of shoulders and the sudden sucking in of breath; or it is written in the book of the intermediaries, those who will spend the next ten days in a state of suspended judgment, in the process of transformation, after which they will be entered into one of the other two books. All of a sudden you hear your own name being called, and you want to cry out, No! No! No! Not now! I didn't realize this was real. I thought this was just some empty ritual. I am completely unprepared. I thought it was just what came after dinner with my family. Please give me some more time. Let me do something to affect the outcome of all this. But the voice continues to intone your name and there is a rustling of the pages of the books, and your heart is gripped with terror as you wait to see in which one your name will be inscribed.

Maybe you have just walked in cold and are now caught completely by surprise, or maybe you are not completely unprepared. Maybe you began your preparations the Saturday night before at midnight, when the Selichot service was recited. Maybe you have thought a little about this night since then. Or maybe you have even taken this day quite seriously and prepared for it for a long time. Maybe you began seven weeks ago, at Tisha B'Av, using that occasion, which stands for our estrangement from God, to contemplate the nature of your own estrangement from God, your estrangement from yourself, from the people you love, and from Judaism. And then maybe when the shofar blew for the first time, exactly one month ago on Rosh Chodesh Elul, you followed the advice of the rabbis and set aside time every day to contemplate your circumstances, to take stock of yourself in preparation for this critical moment. Maybe you meditated every day during this period. Maybe you came to daily minyan and heard the shofar sound every morning there. Maybe you put your head down on your arm every morning during tachanun — *the prayer of fervent supplication* — *and prayed fiercely. Maybe you prayed more fiercely than you have ever prayed in your life. Maybe you prayed that you might finally overcome yourself and experience real transformation, that you might finally get a handle on the suf-*

fering — on the pain that has been weighing so hard on your heart for so long, or on the suffering you seem helpless to prevent yourself from inflicting on others. So maybe you walked in cold, or maybe you have been preparing for months, but no matter what, you now realize you are utterly unprepared, and you apple. You choke. You freeze. Whatever it was that you imagined might happen now, this is much stronger, much more powerful. This is no mere metaphor, no mere religious poetry. This is real. This is extremely powerful, and whatever preparation you might have made now seems utterly foolish, utterly inadequate, as the great voice intones your name, and you hear it reverberating in the great room, and the pages of one of the great books begin to rustle, and you don't know which book it is.

On the night my daughter Hannah was born, I was determined that the birth would be a grand spiritual event. We were already somewhat disappointed on this score. We had wanted a home birth, but the doctor had advised against it, fearing that, given Sherril's age — she was a bit older than the standard childbearing age — the risk of complication would be too great. But we were determined to make the best of it anyway, or at least I was. I meditated through the night, and then when Sherril's contractions began to come very close to each other, I intensified my meditation. Sherril, of course, could have cared less. She had enough to concentrate on as it was. I helped her time the contractions and I coached her breathing through them, but I continued to meditate between contractions. And then finally it was time to go off to the hospital. All right, we couldn't have a home birth. But the doctor would deliver the baby in the relative quiet and privacy of a labor room, without bright lights or invasive technologies. I would continue to meditate. We would have a spiritual experience by hook or by crook.

But when we got to the hospital, the actual experience of birth began to take over, and it blew away all my pitiful attempts at preparation like the exceedingly thin reeds that they were. First of all, there were in fact complications. Sherril's water broke, but the labor wasn't progressing quickly enough and the doctors became very concerned. For the first time, the possibility that things might not turn out well began to arise in our extremely naive minds. They wheeled Sherril downstairs for X rays. This terrified both of us. When they brought her back up, they hooked her up to fetal monitors and gave her Pitocin to induce more substantial contractions. The beeping and pulsing of electronic devices now filled the labor room, and more substantial contractions did in fact come, and they came with a vengeance. They were intensely painful, as they often are when induced, and now we were both hanging on for dear life. For the first and only time in our relationship, Sherril spoke unlovingly to me. When I reached out to try to comfort her during a particularly excruciating contraction, she screamed, "Don't touch me!" I was crushed. My dreams of a spiritual experience had now completely evaporated, and I saw them clearly for the foolishness they had always been. My own wife hated me, her life and the life of our new baby were now both in peril, and we were both completely terrified. Now the doctor informed us that things were getting so dicey that they had decided not to try to have the birth in the quiet and privacy of the labor room, but rather to wheel Sherril into the formal delivery room, where all the latest medical technology would be available to them. Frankly, they now felt they needed all the help they could get.

So they wheeled Sherril into the delivery room. She was grimacing horribly and focusing on her breathing with everything she had. I followed along behind, crestfallen and deeply anxious, my heart full of terror and utterly broken. And it was at that precise moment that God put in an appearance in the delivery room. It was Friday at sundown, and the last thing I saw through a window in the hallway before I went into the delivery room was the sun of Shabbat going down behind Mount St. Helena. There was a huge round lamp at the center of the delivery room ceiling. It gave the room a kind of spiraled spirituality, a radiance. When the birth itself occurred, the room was full of every kind of bodily fluid imaginable, the most intense breathing I have ever witnessed, the skilled movements of the doctors, the nurses, and the mother, and the presence of God. The presence of God was so thick, and so real, and so absolutely connected to the pain and the anxiety and the biological trauma of birth, that the fantasy of birth I had first envisioned now seemed downright stupid.

And maybe that's how you feel right now, if you think you have been preparing for this event for months, but walk in here to find the reality of Rosh Hashanah is making a mockery of these preparations, exposing them for the thin and inadequate reeds that they are. You feel devastated. You feel stupid. All those hours of practice, and now your name has been called and you are standing on the stage choking away like a champ. You can't remember one thing you resolved to do. You try to recall your idea of what this should feel like, but it all seems so small and so thin next to this immense and pulsing reality, next to your name being called and the pages rustling in a book that might mean death or might mean life.

—

And here is the bad news I have come to deliver. This is a true story, and it is not about me or my mother or a man desperate to blow the shofar. It is about you. It is really happening, and it is happening to you, and you are seriously unprepared.

And it is real whether you believe in God or not. Perhaps God made it real and perhaps God did not. Perhaps God created this pageant of judgment and choice, of transformation, of life and of death. Perhaps God created the Book of Life and the Book of Death, Teshuvah and the blowing of the shofar. Or perhaps these are all just inventions of human culture. It makes no difference. It is equally real in any case. The weeks and the months and the years are also inventions of human culture. Time and biology are inventions of human culture. Language and stories, love and tragedy, are inventions of human culture. But they are all matters of life and death, all real and all inescapable. Even though we invented the idea of weeks, we die when our allotted number of weeks has gone by. So if this event is merely the product of human culture, it is the product of an exceedingly rich culture, one that has been accumulating focus and force for three thousand years.

Or perhaps God made the reality that all this human culture seeks to articulate. Perhaps God made a profoundly mixed world, a world in which every second confronts us with a choice between blessings and curses, life and death; a world in which our choices have indelible consequences; a world in which life and death, blessings and curses, choose us, seek us, find us every moment. And we live with the consequences of our choices. And perhaps we have chosen arbitrary spiritual language to express these things, or perhaps God made human culture so that we would express these things precisely as we have in every detail. It makes no difference.

—

What makes a difference is that it's real and it is happening right now and it is happening to us, and it is utterly inescapable, and we are completely unprepared. This moment is before us with its choices, and the consequences of our past choices are before us, as is the possibility of our transformation. This year some of us will die, and some of us will live, and all of us will change.

And there is nothing in the world more real than this. Rabbi Akiva used to say everything is given on pledge and a net is spread for all the living. The store is open and the storekeeper allows credit. The ledger is open and the hand writes. Whoever wishes to borrow may come and borrow, but the collectors go around and exact payment whether we realize it or not.

And maybe it is inescapable because God has made it so, because it is part of some divinely ordained scheme. Or maybe it is merely inescapably fixed by the endless and ageless web of Jewish religious culture — the nascent eruption of these ideas in the Bible, and their subsequent reinterpretation in the Talmud, and their loving elaboration at the hands of the medieval liturgists. The month of Elul, Selichot, the endlessly rich liturgy of the Rosh Hashanah Musaf (additional) service, the blowing of the shofar, the Torah readings and the readings from the Prophets, the liturgical insertions for the Ten Days, Kol Nidre, Yom Kippur and its unique liturgy, its unique Musaf, Mincah, Maftir Yonah, and that last, desperate moment at Neilah, when we are all crushed together so desperately, shuddering at the final closing of the gates — all of it accumulating for thousands of years, until we are inexorably hammered into this moment of inescapable existential choice, life and death, good and evil. And this is an immense reality, and all our resolutions and strategies for coping, all our attempts to manipulate reality, all our attempts to get cute with life, are thin reeds in the face of this immensity. Even if we've spent months preparing, when we reach this moment, we realize we are utterly unprepared.

And this is what we call heartbreak. Heartbreak is precisely the feeling that we have done our best, we have given it our all, but it hasn't been enough. Not nearly enough. And this is what we mean when we say, "God is close to the brokenhearted." And this is what we mean when we say *ain banu ma'asim* — we have no good deeds. This is what it says in "Avinu Malkenu," that lovely song with the haunting, heartbreaking melody we all love to sing so much on Rosh Hashanah. *Avinu malkenu, chanenu v'anenu* — Our Father, our King, be gracious to us, be gratuitously loving, and answer us even though we don't deserve it — *ki ain banu ma'asim* — because we have no good deeds to invoke in our own defense. In other words, now that we are standing in the face of this immense reality, we realize that there is nothing we can do about it; that all our deeds are as nothing. We realize that we have greatly overestimated our cleverness and our potency; we have overestimated the efficacy of our conscious behavior, and we have underestimated the persistence and the depth of our destructive tendencies. We realize that our attempts to do good are very small next to the unconscious havoc we constantly wreak to our right and to our left. "What are we? What is our life? What is our goodness? What our righteousness?" asks the prayer we recite each morning at Shacharit.

> Master of all worlds, it is not on account of our own righteousness that we offer supplications before you, but rather, on account of your great compassion. What are we? What is our life? What is our goodness? What our righteousness?

What is our helpfulness? What our might? What can we say in your presence, Lord, our God and God of our fathers? Indeed, all our mightiest people are as nothing before you, our people of renown as though they never existed, the wise as if they knew nothing, the intelligent as if they understood nothing, for most of our doings are worthless, and the days of our lives are vain in your sight. Our imagined superiority to the beast is just an illusion, and everything we do is just a passing breath.

There was a time when our biblical ancestors thought they really had things figured out. They thought they knew what to do. They thought they had life under control. All they had to do was to make the prescribed sacrifices at the Great Temple in Jerusalem and everything would be taken care of, everything would be all right. But then they ran into the immense wall of reality, and they saw what a thin reed this idea was. And it makes no difference how we understand that immensity. If you were a biblical Prophet, the immensity was the social reality of the day. People were starving, people were homeless, strangers and orphans and widows were uncared for. The sacrifices, the rituals of the Temple, were a very thin reed in the face of this immensity, and the Prophets told us so. And if you were a rabbi of the talmudic era, you saw this immensity in theological terms. The sacrificial cult was a thin reed next to Israel's apostasy at the time of the First Temple, and the rampant, baseless hatred that prevailed at the time of the Second. And if you are a modern historian, then the immensity was a simple historical one. The sacrificial cult was an exceedingly thin reed next to the invincible might of the Roman army that

destroyed everything in its path and would have destroyed Jerusalem and the Temple no matter how well we had taken care of
the helpless in our midst, no matter how pious we had been, no
matter how loving we had been to one another. So it makes little
difference how we view this immensity, the point is, *ain banu
ma'asim* — we have no good deeds. We thought we knew what to
do, we thought we had things figured out, but then we ran into the
wall of reality. We turned around and saw an immense crowd
looking back at us at Carnegie Hall. We suddenly found ourselves
in the presence of an immense being, the master of the Holy
Name. We were suddenly hooked up to fetal monitors, suddenly
wheeled into the operating room, and we appled. We choked. We
understood that all our preparations had been inadequate — that
the reality we now confronted was so powerful and irresistible that
it had blown all our attempts to prepare for it away like so many
chaffs of straw. The sacrificial cult was over, the audience was fil-
ing out of Carnegie Hall, the birth was under way, and all those
hours of meditation and prayer and practice now seemed like a
cruel joke. The Temple was destroyed. The walls of the city had
crumbled.

This is what we call heartbreak. This is why I always feel that
the High Holidays start at Tisha B'Av, the day when we mourn
the fall of the Temple, the day precisely seven weeks before Rosh
Hashanah when we begin our preparations for reconciliation
with God by acknowledging our estrangement from God. This
is the day when the walls come tumbling down and we begin to
acknowledge our heartbreak, when we begin to acknowledge the
futility of our present course of action, when we begin to acknowledge the fact that we are utterly unprepared for what we have

THIS IS REAL AND YOU ARE COMPLETELY UNPREPARED

to face in life. This is when the walls of our psyche begin to break down.

And then comes Elul, and with these walls already down we try to see our real circumstances, we try to see who we really are and what we really have. We try to acknowledge the emptiness of what we have been doing.

And then Rosh Hashanah itself arrives, and perhaps this is the beginning of the process for you, or perhaps this is its culmination, or perhaps you are somewhere in between. But wherever you are in this, this much is sure: *ain banu ma'asim* — you have no good deeds. You are utterly unprepared. Nothing you have done or can do has had or will have any efficacy at all.

So what do we do at a moment like this, when we become so painfully aware that there is nothing we can do at all?

The Midrash from Tanna D'Veit Eliyuahu Zuta with which we began is quite explicit. We do three things. And the good news after all this very bad news is that we already know how to do them. In fact, we do them every year at the High Holidays.

꙰ **The first thing** we do during the High Holidays is come together; we stand together before God as a single spiritual unit. We do this out of a very deep instinct. Just stand out on the street in front of the synagogue and try to stop people from coming into our services and you will see the great force of this incredible instinct Jews have to be together with other Jews at this moment. They have no tickets, they never even called, but just try to stop them and you will feel the force of this instinct. We need each other now. We need each other deeply. Here in the full flush of the reality of the life-and-death nature of this ritual, here in the full flush of our impotence as individuals to meet this most urgent emergency, our need for each other is immense. We heal one another by being together. We give each other hope. Now we know for sure — by ourselves, *ain banu ma'asim,* there is nothing we can do. But gathered together as a single indivisible entity, we sense that we do in fact have efficacy as a larger, transcendent spiritual unit, one that has been expressing meaning and continuity for three thousand years, one that includes everyone who is here, and everyone who is not here, to echo the phrase we always read in the Torah the week before the High Holidays begin — all those who came before us, and all those who are yet to come, all those who are joined in that great stream of spiritual consciousness from which we have been struggling to know God for thousands of years. We now stand in that stream, and that is the first thing we do.

And then second, *v'hitvadu* — we make confession. We open our hearts. We acknowledge the futility of our actions. We see our attempts to be cute with this life, to manipulate it, for the thin reeds they are, and we resolve to give them up. And we are able to find the courage to do this precisely because we are gathered *ba'agudat achat* — in one single spiritual unit — precisely because we now realize that the enterprise doesn't depend on our own single, puny, thin, pale stratagems, but on our belonging to something much larger and deeper and thicker than that.

And third, we perform this service, this ancient ritual of judgment and transformation, of forgiveness, of life and death. We perform it because we got it from God. God came out of the mist and the mystery. God donned a tallit and passed before the ark. God dressed himself in the implements of human culture and revealed this service to us through our own evolution as a people.

So on the first night of Rosh Hashanah, there we are, *ba'agudat achat,* pressed together in a large room, a single spiritual unit, helping each other to acknowledge our actual condition, and reciting this ancient service given to us by the Divine Physician as a medicine for that condition, and that condition is this:

This is real. This is very real.

This is absolutely inescapable.

And we are utterly unprepared.

And we have nothing to offer but each other and our broken hearts.

And that will be enough.

CHAPTER SIX

THE HORN BLOWS,
THE GATES SWING OPEN,
AND WE FEEL
THE WINDS OF HEAVEN

ROSH HASHANAH

*THE THREE BOOKS ARE OPENED IN HEAVEN. WHEN THE
shofar sounds one hundred times, it blows open the gates of
heaven. When the shofar sounds one hundred times, it forms a
bridge between heaven and earth, and we enter heaven on that
bridge. When the shofar blows one hundred times, it cracks the
shell of our awareness wide open, and suddenly we find ourselves in heaven. When the shofar blows one hundred times, we
hear the voice of heaven in it. We experience Revelation. God's
voice comes down to earth on the same bridge we used to go up to
heaven. On Rosh Hashanah, all the inhabitants of the earth
pass before God in heaven. Rosh Hashanah is Yom Harat Ha-
Olam — the Day the World Is Born; the day heaven gives birth
to the earth. Rosh Hashanah is Yom Ha-Zikaron — the Day of*

Remembrance; the day we remember that our roots are in heaven, the day heaven remembers us. Rosh Hashanah is the day of kingship, the day we acknowledge the sovereignty of heaven over our earthly lives.

In the Une Tane Tokef prayer, the liturgical high point of both the Rosh Hashanah and Yom Kippur services, the curtains between heaven and earth are pulled back and we catch a glimpse of the celestial mechanics that govern the earth. In this prayer we acknowledge the awesome power of this day, its pure sanctity, the deeply felt dominion of heaven, the heavenly roots of Compassion and Justice.

This day, even angels are alarmed, seized with fear and trembling as they declare: "The day of judgment is here!" for even the hosts of heaven are judged, and this day, all who walk the earth are brought before You. . . . You determine the life and decree the destiny of every creature.

On Rosh Hashanah it is written and on Yom Kippur it is sealed, how many will leave this world and how many will be born into it, who will live and who will die, who will live out the limits of their days and who will not, who will perish by fire and who by water, who by sword and who by beast, who by hunger and who by thirst. Who by earthquake and who by plague, who will rest and who will wander, who will be poor and who will be rich, who will be humbled and who will be exalted. But Teshuvah and Prayer and Righteous Acts transform the severity, the evil of the decree.

As the Une Tane Tokef closes, we are reminded once again of the vast gulf separating our earthly existence from the heavenly expanse we glimpse on Rosh Hashanah.

—

Our origin is dust and our end is dust. We spend our life earning bread. We are like a clay vessel easily broken, like the withering grass, like a fading flower, a passing shadow, a fugitive cloud, a fleeting breeze, scattering dust, a vanishing dream, BUT YOU ARE KING, ETERNAL GOD. Your years have no limit, Your days have no end, Your sublime glory is beyond comprehension, Your mysterious name is beyond explanation.

If we have been paying attention for the past seven weeks, none of this should come as a surprise. At Tisha B'Av we became aware of our brokenness; during Elul we cultivated an awareness of our actual circumstances, the dust we will return to, the fragility and impermanence of our life. If we succeeded in awakening to our lives we saw clearly how every moment of our lives, every breath, every thought, is only a passing shadow, a fugitive cloud, a fleeting breeze, a vanishing dream. This being the case, how do we acquire a toehold in this world sufficient to do Teshuvah? How do we achieve the transformation our contemplation has shown us we need to make? As Selichot dawns, there is a sense of urgency, even desperation, about our plight, but we have also become aware of the limits of our own powers. We are completely unprepared for this. We don't know how to do Teshuvah. We are incapable of transforming ourselves.

For this, we need to enter a realm beyond the one we usually occupy, a consciousness beyond our own. For this, we need the limitless, the endless, the incomprehensible, the measureless, the mysterious. In short, we need heaven. This is where Rosh Hashanah carries us.

Something very strange happens to the Torah just before Rosh Hashanah. It disappears from the weekly services, as if it has fallen into a void. The Torah is read in a cycle of weekly readings that is both completed and begun again on Simchat Torah, the last day of the festival of Sukkot, some ten days after Yom Kippur. Toward the end of the cycle, Moses dies a noble and tragic death, poised on the border of the Promised Land he will never enter. Then the round of weekly Torah readings halts and remains suspended for several weeks until the long round of holidays — Rosh Hashanah, Yom Kippur, Sukkot, Shemini Atseret, and Simchat Torah — is completed. Then suddenly the Torah begins again in a great rush with the first strains of Genesis and its account of creation. Life bursts into being out of nothing, out of the void the Torah had fallen into after the death of Moses.

There is something of this feeling about Rosh Hashanah as well. Rosh Hashanah is, among other things, Yom Harat Ha-Olam — the Day the World Is Born. Rosh Hashanah is also the day that the world burst into being out of nothing, and it stands for both that event and its continuous renewal. Every moment of our lives the world bursts into being out of nothing, falls away, and then rises up again. Every moment we are renewed by a plunge into the void. This void is called heaven.

There is a void at the beginning of creation and a void afterward. Life is the narrow bridge between these two emptinesses. Usually all our focus is on the narrow bridge of our own life, rather than on what comes before or after. In its accounts of both the death of Moses and the creation of the universe, the Torah focuses our attention instead on the void.

One Sunday morning the first summer I was a rabbi in San Francisco, I received two phone calls within moments of each other. The first concerned a death that had just occurred on Twenty-seventh Avenue on the north side of Golden Gate Park, and the second concerned a birth that had just occurred on Twenty-seventh Avenue on the south side of the same park. I was struck by the coincidence of events — this life and this death taking place at opposite ends of the same street at almost the same moment, and I spoke of it often from the pulpit; and when I did, I focused on the events themselves — the birth and the death. I spoke of how the simultaneity of these two events seemed to symbolize the Jewish view of life as a whole system, a richness in which birth and death are in equilibrium, at either end of a con tinuum. My wife, the author Sherril Jaffe, was also impressed by this experience, but when she wrote about it in her novel *Interior Designs*, her focus was quite different. She said:

> These things are on the same continuum, but there is a park in between, a wild and beautiful place without streets and numbers. Flowers bloom there, and there are lakes where egrets wade. The cypresses are dark and cool. It is a beautiful place, as large and deep as a dream. But I hurry through there almost daily on my way to and from the places where the streets are numbered.

Like the Torah, Sherril focused not on the events of this world, not on birth and not on death, but on the void in between, and she found this nothingness to be a wild, fecund place, a place we don't notice in our fascination with the world of things and numbers. The Kabala also points to a wild and fecund nothingness at the core of existence. According to the Kabala, before creation there was nothing but heaven. God existed as the Ain Sof, the Endlessness, an emptiness so charged, so powerful, that nothing could coexist with it. In order to create the universe, God had to extract the Divine Essence from a tiny sphere at the center of the Ain Sof. This sphere became the known universe. But the point is, the universe came out of nothing. It was born from an endless emptiness. Or as my grandmother Masha used to say, in a pungent paraphrase of a saying from the Talmud, "You come out of one black hole and you go into another."

This is the account of the Torah as well. According to the Torah, human life emerged from *tohu v'vohu* — a howling, empty chaos — and the medium of its creation was *ruach elohim* — the divine breath, wind and air, nothingness in motion — by which a lump of dust and earth was transformed into a *nefesh chaim* — a living soul. But the word *nefesh*, soul, also means a nothingness. It also means air or breath. Breath — *ruach, nefesh* — is precisely an energized nothingness, a dynamic emptiness at the center of our being that mirrors the dynamic emptiness out of which life arose.

But there is another, somewhat darker sense in which this world seems to have arisen out of nothing.

Earlier I mentioned *The Denial of Death,* by the philosopher Ernest Becker, and Becker's observation that we human beings seem to be the only creatures afflicted with the mysterious capacity to understand that we are going to die, and that it is precisely this fact that seems to call us to the world, to our life's work, and to God. We try to compensate for this dread intelligence by constructing what Becker calls affirmation systems. We see the void and it terrifies us; it looks to us like utter negation. So we try to set up something in life that affirms our existence.

Against death, which we see as the ultimate failure, we offer up success.

Against death, which we see as the ultimate emptiness, we offer up the acquisition of objects.

Against death, which we see as the end of all feeling, we offer up the pursuit of pleasure.

Against death, which we see as the final stillness, we offer up a ceaseless rage of activity.

Against death, which we see as the ultimate impotence, we offer up the glorification of our own power.

But in the process, we give up our nefesh — the nothingness out of which life arises, the emptiness that gives our lives meaning. And we give it up because we are frightened of it. It reeks of all we are trying to deny. Consequently, we've become a nation of workaholics, a people who have come to believe that we can conquer death by dint of our own powers, by a ceaseless swirl of activity. To rest is to die, so we never permit ourselves a moment's rest, a moment's nefesh, a moment's nothingness. We think we know how the world works. We think we even know how the mind works. We have become enchanted with how capable we've become with our computers, our jet planes, our space travel, our genetic engineering. We've talked ourselves into believing that we can solve any problem, overcome any obstacle if we just do more, if we just think about it long and hard enough, if we just try a little harder.

But our problem is not that we don't try hard enough. It is that we try too hard. It's that we have such an exaggerated belief in the force of our own effort that we never stop trying. Our pursuit of pleasure and success is relentless, feverish, sometimes bordering on the demonic. We never rest. We have portable computers and faxes and e-mail that we take on vacation. We have phones in our cars. We have call waiting, so that even our interruptions are interrupted. Even those small moments of contemplation — of nefesh, of nothingness — we used to enjoy on vacation or even just driving back and forth between errands, even these are denied us.

But in spite of our constant effort, there is failure and death all around us, on the downtown streets and in the testimony of our own bodies. We try not to see it, but the psychic squint we have to make in order to do this reduces everything in our line of sight, not just the void we are trying to ignore. And this squinting requires a tremendous expenditure of energy, energy we desperately need, and it never works anyway. Sooner or later we will find ourselves tied to a chair under the bare bulb of the truth.

Sexually, physically, and mentally, we humans peak in our early twenties. After that we decline. Our heart muscles weaken and we lose stamina and endurance. Our blood pressure increases and our arteries harden, and this affects our brain, heart, kidneys, and the extremities, and none of them take it well. The gastrointestinal system also begins to slow. The prostate enlarges. Our hormones slow to a trickle, making us look older and feel less energy and initiative. Our bones leach calcium and phosphates and become fragile. The skin thins, dries, and becomes discolored. Our brain atrophies. Our nerve cells waste away. We suffer memory loss, sometimes severe. Birth is our only real success, and even that success doesn't really belong to us. It belongs to God. In the beginning, God created us out of nothing. It is all downhill from there, and that's the part that belongs to us — the long, slow return to nothing.

——

But if we stop resisting it for a moment, it is precisely this return that can save us. It is precisely this return that can renew us, return us to heaven.

Human renewal is one of the universe's great mysteries, one we tend to take for granted. When our cars run out of gas, we fill them up with gas. When our batteries run down, we recharge them with electrical energy. But when we human beings run down, we simply plunge into nothingness. We sleep. Nothing happens to us when we sleep, and it is precisely this nothing that restores us.

When we lose touch with this sense of nefesh, of space, of emptiness, we feel overwhelmed, overstressed, overburdened. So for many of us the question is, How do we find our way back to heaven? How do we relocate that spaciousness out of which we emerged? How do we connect with our nefesh?

There is a story in the Torah about someone getting their nefesh back, although I use the word "someone" advisedly, because the someone in question is God. After six furious days of creating the world, the Torah says of God, *Shavat vayinafash* — God stopped and did nothing, or literally, God stopped and re-nefeshed himself, re-ensouled himself. So we get back to heaven by doing nothing. We reconnect with the nothing that gives our life meaning by stopping.

The Torah has another word for this nothingness which also permeates the Rosh Hashanah liturgy, and that is the word *kadosh*, or holy. The angels cry out, *Kadosh*, as they circle the heavenly throne. It is used for the first time in reference to Shabbat, that sacred stopping. After that, *kadosh* fills the Torah, and the imperative of the Torah is that we fill the world with holiness as well.

—

Holiness is the great nothing that appears in all the religious traditions of the world in various poetic guises. It is an ineffable intensity, an oceanic sense, a warm flash of light, a marriage of the soul, a mighty wind of resolution, a starry grace, a burning bush, a wide-stretching love, an abyss of pure simplicity, and as we have mentioned, it is the word the angels cry, the word that rings throughout heaven.

In short, holiness is an all-encompassing emptiness. In short, holiness is heaven. And Rosh Hashanah is about our connection to heaven. Rebbe Nachman of Bratslav said that when the shofar blows one hundred times on Rosh Hashanah, a bridge is formed between heaven and earth. And those mysterious, otherworldly sounds the shofar makes are a secret language that is understood only in heaven, according to the Tiferet Uziel. Rosh Hashanah is the day we are remembered in heaven, as God remembers Sarah in the Torah reading we read on the first day of the holiday. And the story of the Akeda — the Binding of Isaac — that we read on the second day, affirms the covenant between Abraham and God, that indissoluble connection between heaven and earth. When we pray for forgiveness on Rosh Hashanah, we do so not on the basis of our merits, which we realize are woefully inadequate, but on the strength of that connection.

"Lord of the Worlds!" we pray on that morning.

Not upon our merit do we rely in supplication, but upon Your boundless compassion. What are we? What is our piety? What is our righteousness? What is our attainment, our power, our might? What can we say to You? All the mighty are as nothing; the famous, as if they didn't exist; the wise, utterly lacking in wisdom. The greatest part of our actions are utterly meaningless, the days of our lives an emptiness, our superiority over the beast is an illusion. Our life is a fleeting breath. But we are Your people, Your partners, connected to You by the covenant.

Without this connection to heaven, we can't make Teshuvah. We can't forgive others or ourselves without it. We can't see ourselves without it. We can't know ourselves. These things are simply too difficult to do. Our capacities, our vision, our powers, our tolerance for pain, are too limited; our capacity for self-deception and rationalization too persistent.

Recently a young man came to see me in my office seeking advice. He had been in a relationship with a wonderful young woman for several years. She was beautiful and kind and he was very fond of her. His family loved her and was urging him to marry her. She also wanted to marry, but he found himself balking. He thought he might love her, but he didn't feel challenged by her. She had unquestioningly adopted every idea he had ever expressed as her own. She had changed her life to adapt to his, but she had never asked him to change for her sake in any way. It worried him that she never seemed able to discuss the things that were important to him. She simply wasn't a big talker. She was a nourisher. She supported every idea he ever had. She adopted his lifestyle as her own. His brother told him, You're an idiot. Marry her right away. You'll never have it this good again. His parents told him, She's so sweet. She's so beautiful. She loves you so much. What are you waiting for? But he worried that she wasn't really his soul mate. He wondered if he shouldn't be with someone

—

who pushed him a bit more, who brought more of herself to the relationship.

This worry became a kind of torment. He thought about it constantly. Was he just resisting commitment? Was he afraid of intimacy, of giving up his independence? If so, he would be glad to give up this resistance, but how could he be sure? Perhaps this really wasn't the right relationship for him. Perhaps this woman, as lovely and as loving as she was, was not his true partner, the one with whom he was destined to spend his life. But how could he know for sure? Was this the authentic resistance of his soul, or was he just a big kid who refused to grow up?

I didn't know the answer, I told him, and neither did he. He was disappointed with my first point but certainly agreed with the second. Who does know the answer? I asked him. The question hung in the air between us for a long, pregnant moment, before the obvious answer presented itself, coalescing on the ether, like a colloid suspension suddenly taking form. God knew the answer to this question. I didn't know it and neither did the young man, but God knew it. And the answer would not come through effort. It would not come through exertion. It would not come through filling the mind up with reasons and arguments. It would only come when his mind was empty. It would only come from heaven. It would only come after his question was cast into the void — the great nothingness at the core of this young man's being. It would only come if he asked God for it. And it might have to hang suspended between heaven and earth for a long time before it began to take form.

One summer, after a very stressful year — problems in the congregation, financial crises, illness, conflict, and trouble — Sherril and I took a vacation to a small, deserted town by the sea. There was absolutely nothing to do — no phone, no television, no movies — and as the days stretched on, we began to notice a strange sensation. At first I thought it was just the humid ocean air, but then we realized it wasn't the air that had taken on a dimension of depth, it was the time. The time seemed to have thickened and deepened. And our feelings for each other, buried for so long under so much activity and stress, began to emerge full throttle. We felt as if all the nothing — the sudden absence of activity, phones, TV — all this nothing had healed us. We had stopped, we had plunged into nothingness, and we had been re-ensouled.

On Rosh Hashanah, the gates between heaven and earth are opened, and things that were beyond us suddenly become possible. The deepest questions of our heart begin to find answers. Our deepest fear, that gaping emptiness up ahead of us and back behind us as well, suddenly becomes our ally. Heaven begins to help us.

⁂

I was sitting in my living room alone one Saturday afternoon, when I heard the sound of a basketball bouncing on the sidewalk outside. Before I knew it, big, wet tears started rolling down my cheeks. The sound of the ball took me back to when I used to shoot hoops with my father, now dead fourteen years. We played on the little asphalt court he built for me down the hill from our house. I was an American kid. I lived for sports. I was captain of my high school football team, and I had all the moves in basketball. I could dribble behind my back. I could shoot the J. But my father was born in Poland to a family of war refugees, and when he came to America at the age of nine, he spent every afternoon of his young life working to help support his family. So my father couldn't shoot the J; my father didn't have any moves. My father would fling the ball wildly toward the basket like a shot-putter gone berserk. When he tried to dribble, the ball would go bounding off in every direction.

Now you should know that my father had an ego as big as all New York; he never admitted he was wrong, and he competed fiercely at everything he did. He defended his position in the silliest argument as if his life depended on it. Yet he regularly humiliated himself by coming down to this asphalt court to shoot baskets with me, laughing at his own ineptitude, cackling with self-deprecation as the ball flew out of his hands as if it had a will of its own. I never realized it then, but it seems obvious now that he only came down to be with me, his real live American kid, whom he must have loved as desperately as I love my own children today.

And as I sat in the living room that Shabbat, I realized something else I hadn't realized before: my father was about as beautiful as it is possible for a human being to be down there on that basketball court. It was the only time I ever knew him to be comfortable saying, "This is me. With all my limitations, with all the loss and suffering my life has dealt me, this is exactly who I am." Sitting there in the living room, I could see that radiant, open, laughing face of his, a face transformed by self-forgiveness. That was when the tears came.

Self-forgiveness is the essential act of the High Holiday season. That's why we need heaven. That's why we need God. We can forgive others on our own. But we turn to God, Rabbi Eli Spitz reminds us, because we cannot forgive ourselves. We need to feel judged and accepted by a Power who transcends our limited years and who embodies our highest values. When we wish to wipe the slate clean, to finalize self-forgiveness, we need heaven — a sense of something or someone larger and beyond our self.

Though self-forgiveness may end with God, it begins with us. Self-forgiveness is difficult largely because we hold ourselves to such high standards, higher than it is possible to live up to. And it is precisely when we are hardest on ourselves that we are most tempted to bury our misdeeds — to hide from our reality, to deny weakness, to deny that we've done anything wrong.

The relentlessness of the High Holidays — the long days in synagogue, the constant repetition of the prayers, the fasting — wears down our defenses and helps us open to the truth of our lives. The aspect of the High Holidays that is most helpful in this regard is their holiness. The sense of the sacred is attenuated in the modern world, to say the least. Still, these are and have never stopped being the High *Holy* Days, the Days of Awe, the days that convey a quality of holiness we can all feel, even if we feel it only dimly. It is precisely this holiness that helps us forgive ourselves. These days create a context of holiness, and if we pay close attention, we begin to notice that everything in our lives is suffused with holiness, even those "faults" we thought we had to forgive ourselves for. Even that behavior we took to be wrongful, we now realize, has a holy spark at its center waiting to be released. This is the essence of self-forgiveness.

Rabbi and contemporary mystic Lawrence Kushner writes,

We may go down into ourselves with a flashlight, looking for the evil we have intended or done — not to excise it as some alien growth, but rather to discover the holy spark within it. Rabbi Yakov Yosef of Polnoye taught: The essence of the finest Teshuvah (the return to one's Source in Heaven) is that deliberate sins are transformed into merits. So it was that the Ba'al Shem Tov interpreted the verse from Proverbs, "Turn aside from evil and do good" to mean "Turn evil into good."

Inner healing requires self-acceptance. Rebbe Nachman of Bratslav offered the following strategy: When all we see and feel is negativity, we must search within ourselves for an aspect of goodness, what he called a white dot within the black, and then find another and another until these dots form musical notes. Our task, he said, is to find enough white notes to form a melody — a melody that will define our core and affirm our fundamental goodness.

The Talmud tells us that in the world to come, everyone will be called to account for all the desires they might have fulfilled in this world but chose not to. The things we desire — the desires themselves — are sacred. Who put them in our hearts if not God? But we have been taught to be ashamed of what we want; our desires become horribly distorted and cause us to do terribly hurtful things. Even a betrayal as painful as adultery might turn out to have its roots in a perfectly innocent desire — in the desire to be loved, to have our experience be intense and exciting — and if we could acknowledge these innocent desires, we might not feel compelled to act them out in such hurtful ways.

—

The same is true of the desire for fame and success. We are conditioned to think that it is wrong to want these things, to be too ambitious. And the truth is, we do often end up injuring both ourselves and others in pursuit of these desires. But underneath them may be the perfectly legitimate, even laudable, need to use our God-given abilities to the utmost. The same God who gave us these abilities also gave us the desire to use them to their fullest capacity.

Our desires are neither base nor sinful in and of themselves. They are implanted in us by God to carry us along in our lives, to propel us down the path we need to follow. And if we could accept them as such, we probably wouldn't need to stab our best friend in the back or sleep with our wife's best friend.

Ray, our family cat, was a stray who showed up at our house on the weekend of Parshat Re'eh, thus his name. Eventually we adopted him, and he is still with us some fifteen years later. My daughters, ages six and five at the time, were ecstatic. My wife was not. She was worried that the cat would eat the current family pets, a pair of guinea pigs named Bennie and Bert. Her concern seemed irrational to me. Paranoid.

"Why would the cat want to eat the guinea pigs?" I wanted to know. It seemed to me it would be the farthest thing from his mind. "Because that's the way cats are," Sherril replied. "They're predators." And in that moment I was struck to the root with the realization of what a miracle it is that everything on this planet — animal, vegetable, and mineral — is made a particular way. We are also made a particular way. Okay, maybe it is not in our nature to attack guinea pigs. But the way we are is sacred nevertheless. To forgive ourselves, we must be willing to give up our ideas about how we might be better.

We need to give up one of our most cherished beliefs — that there is something wrong with us, that we are bad, inadequate, somehow defective and lacking in goodness. Disciplining ourselves, rejecting ourselves, beating ourselves, leads us farther away from this goodness, not closer to it.

"If I have an idea about how I should be (more compassionate, for example), and I go through a process of rejecting myself every time I don't meet this standard, I will never find that compassion," the Buddhist teacher Sharon Salzberg writes. One kind of emotional process cannot possibly produce another kind of emotional process. Rejection will not lead to compassion. Only compassion can lead to compassion. Rejection will only lead to rejection.

But what would happen if every time we did something we disapproved of, we opened our heart to heaven? What would happen if every time we felt an impulse we didn't like, we acknowledged its Divine origin? This may be the only change we really need to undertake.

The Talmud originally taught that when we pray, and do Teshuvah and Tzedakah (charity), during the ten days between Rosh Hashanah and Yom Kippur, we actually succeed in having the Divine decree against us torn up — *ma'akirin et ha-gezerah*. The terrible things we did are as if they never happened, and their consequences won't happen either.

But do prayer, Teshuvah, and Tzedakah actually change our fate? The rabbis who came along later realized that of course they do not. The real change is in the way we perceive the world. So they changed the language of the prayer accordingly. Now we say, Teshuvah, Tzedakah, and Tefilah *ma'avirin et ro-at ha-gezerah*. The act of Teshuvah is no longer seen as ripping up the evil decree. Now it transforms the evil of the decree. Teshuvah doesn't change what happens, and it doesn't change the way we are. It merely changes the way we see these things. We no longer see things as evil, we simply see them as they are, and that makes all the difference.

Think about the thing you hate about yourself the most. Is it that you're too fat, too weak, too mean? Do you go around talking compulsively behind other people's backs? Do you lie to people? Are you terrible at sports?

What would happen if instead of running away from these perceived weaknesses, you took ownership of them? What if you allowed yourself to inhabit them completely, to crawl inside these traits and fill them up with your being? Please don't misunderstand me. I'm not suggesting that it's all right to keep being mean to people. I am saying that if you keep beating yourself up for being mean, your meanness is just going to keep striking back, getting stronger and more vicious with each blow. If, on the other hand, you were to fill up your meanness with attention and presence, it might just begin to cool down. Like everything else in the world, it will finally have its moment and after that, it will fall away and you won't have to act on it anymore.

The Sabbath is a time when we inhabit ourselves this way. This may be the real reason so few Christians or Jews observe the Sabbath anymore. Work, commerce, and our usual frantic rush of activities are all devices we use to distract ourselves from ourselves, to keep from looking at who we are, to keep us from fully inhabiting our lives. Perhaps the real reason more of us don't observe a

—

Sabbath is not because it's inconvenient — not because we are spiritually lazy — but rather because we are afraid. We are afraid of reflection because we are afraid of ourselves. We are afraid that if we ever stopped running long enough to catch a glimpse of ourselves, we would see something we didn't like.

A few years ago I knew a family who had a teenage boy who was out of control. There was terrible conflict in the family all the time, regular screaming matches, near physical violence. The boy started running away, and eventually his parents saw they had no control over him whatsoever. Now he was out all night. He stopped attending school. They took him to a psychiatrist, and the psychiatrist told them that they were the problem. They didn't know how to enforce consistent discipline — to apply consistent limits. The boy was constantly testing their limits and they were constantly failing these tests, the psychiatrist told them. In fact many people told them this — people at school, friends, acquaintances, people they hardly knew. It had become their mantra, the club of guilt with which they beat themselves black and blue every day. We don't know how to enforce consistent discipline. We don't know how to set consistent limits. So they kept trying to do this, and each attempt was more futile and more disastrous than the last. Each attempt at setting limits, at enforcing discipline, led to uglier confrontations and reenforced the parents' sense of failure. Then the psychiatrist began to suggest that these parents were in over their heads, that they were really not up to being the parents their son needed. He advised them to send the boy away to one of these wilderness camps where rebellious children are taught self-esteem and self-reliance by being exposed to harsh discipline, hard labor, and spartan living conditions. When they told him their son would never agree to go to such a place, he told them that these camps provided "escorts" who would come to your house and pick up your child and accompany him to the camp in restraints if necessary. But they couldn't bring themselves to do this to their boy. It just wasn't in them. This, of course, only made them feel even worse about themselves.

The psychologist at the boy's school also felt they weren't up to the task. He advised them to go to court and have their son declared an emancipated minor, thus placing him on the doorstep of the legal system. This they weren't even tempted to try. So finally, because they had absolutely no alternative whatsoever, they started to look at the reality of their lives a lot more clearly than they had been. The first thing they noticed was that they had absolutely no problem disciplining their other two children when it was necessary, and their other two children were doing fine. Discipline wasn't their problem, they now realized. Their problem was that this boy had a different constitutional makeup. Discipline works very well for some kids, but others internalize it as a devastating and corrosive form of criticism that eats away at their self-esteem. Apparently their son was such a child. So suddenly his parents were able to stop beating up on themselves. They even began to find white spots within the darkness — holy sparks in their son's troubled soul. Their son was a strong-willed, independent young man, full of curiosity about the world, and absolutely unwilling to accept the world on other people's terms. What was so bad about that? Several of these traits, they now realized, came from them. It had taken no small amount of courage for them to follow their own instincts regarding their son and to reject the advice they had been given. Maybe they were not so inadequate as parents after all.

—

Now they dropped all attempts to discipline their son. They tried only to affirm him. He was now out all night almost every night and out of school completely. It was difficult to find anything to affirm, but they persevered. They resisted every impulse to criticize him. They even developed a little ritual. As soon as their son left the house, they would turn to each other and say all the angry things they had wanted to say to him but had wisely restrained themselves from saying. "The reason you don't feel well is because you've been out all night for the past three days," the husband would shout at his wife. "The reason we don't have the food you want here is because you haven't spent enough time at home lately for anyone to have the slightest idea what you want," the wife would shout right back at her husband. Several months passed — difficult, agonizing months. They sometimes wondered if they were being criminally irresponsible and neglectful, but they stayed the course. Then the boy worked his way back to school. Not his old school, but a new school, one he chose. The anger and near violence that had characterized their family life for so long evaporated. The boy began to express affection for his parents. And the last time I spoke to them, the mother was ecstatic. The boy had eaten her food, had actually sat at the family table and dined with his parents for the first time in two years.

The real work we have to do at this time of year, I think, is to find compassion no matter what. But we have to find it for ourselves before we can be of much use to others. The real work is to look at who we really are, and to contemplate Who made us that way.

This I can promise you: neither you nor your children conform to the ideas other people are trying to foist on you. You are the unique creations of God, and any attempt to pin you down to some idea will only diminish you. You are equal to your life. You have been given exactly what you need, not one thing more and not one thing less.

When we experience ourselves exactly as we are, we sense our oneness with everything and we realize there is no such thing as a mistake. When we pay attention, everything enlightens us, even the things we think of as our mistakes. Everything in life comes to us as a teacher — even the sound of a basketball outside our window on Shabbat. There is an old Cherokee proverb: Pay attention, learn quickly. Or as the rabbis used to say: "Who is wise? The person who learns from everyone and everything."

There is a wonderful Midrash in the Talmud about a wicked king named Manasha who lived a full life of evil and cruelty and then made sincere, heartfelt repentance on his deathbed. The Angels of Heaven, who knew that God would forgive Manasha as soon as God heard his repentance, were outraged at the injustice of it all, and they tried to lock the gates of heaven to block out Manasha's words. But God drilled a hole under the Throne of Glory, heard Manasha's confession, and forgave him immediately. Then God turned to the Angels: Look, God said. It's my business to forgive. This is what I do. This is who I am.

Forgiveness — the desire of God to forgive us — is an irresistible force. It fills every space like the waters of a flood. It is one of the most powerful forces on earth, nothing less than the need of the world to be what it is; the need of the universe to have us be what we are. That's why we were created: to be the way we are and not some other way. It is precisely the way we are that is sacred in the first place.

—

135

And it is the nature of God to forgive. This God tells the angels in heaven, and this God tells Moses firsthand in that famous passage from the Torah that is embedded in the High Holiday liturgy. "Show me what You are like," Moses pleads with God, and God complies. "My name is Y-H-V-H. Y-H-V-H. I am gracious and compassionate. I am forgiveness itself." This is the very meaning of my name, God is saying, Y-H-V-H; the verb *to be* in the present tense. I am absolute presence, that aspect of the universe that accepts and forgives.

It is your life's work to turn evil into good. It is your life's work to find the white dots buried within the blackness — and the melody these dots make. This is the melody you were born to dance to. This is the background music for the real life you are living. Listen to it.

What was wrong with my father, for example, was that he couldn't play basketball. He was a poor working stiff, an immigrant without the American graces, and while this may not have been a sin of the magnitude of meanness or infidelity, it was a weakness, and my father did not forgive himself for weaknesses easily. But what was right with him was that he loved his son so much that he managed not to care about this one. He was even willing to forgive himself for his son's sake, and that is the most difficult thing a person can do. It's impossible, in fact, without the help of heaven. I can see him now, in the throes of self-forgiveness, pushing that ball toward the basket, eyes wild and shining, mouth like a fish's, arms akimbo, a foolish grin on his face, dancing with happy abandon between heaven and earth.

On Rosh Hashanah, all who have come into the world pass before God. This statement, which we read in the Mishnah, the earliest stratum of the Talmud, is the first thing our tradition has to say about Rosh Hashanah. Indeed, the idea that God is aware of us, that God sees us and is mindful of us, is the very first assumption of this holy day. In its earlier biblical incarnation, Rosh Hashanah was called Yom Ha-Zikaron, the Day of Remembrance, the Day of Mindfulness. If God were not aware of us, this whole pageant of Teshuvah and forgiveness wouldn't make much sense. Who would there be to return to? How could we ever be forgiven if there weren't an awareness out there that knew precisely what we have done and how we feel about it now? And if Rosh Hashanah did not provide us with the perspective of heaven — with the opportunity to see ourselves with perfect clarity as if from the outside — how would we ever achieve this kind of clarity? How would we ever manage to get far enough outside ourselves to see ourselves accurately?

My great-grandfather Reb Mordecai Shustick was a very close disciple, a Hasid, of the Rhiziner Rebbe. He spent the entire year away from home either studying with his rebbe, or traveling all over Eastern Europe teaching Torah and Talmud from tiny town to tiny town, returning home for only a few days every year to visit his wife and children. On those days, his wife, Chanah, would invariably beg him to have a picture taken. He was home so seldom, she pleaded. His children could barely remember what he looked like. But Reb Mordecai would always refuse. It was forbidden for a Rhiziner Hasid to have his picture taken, and that was that. But one year Chanah prevailed. Everyone in our family has a copy of the resulting photograph. Reb Mordecai looks extremely angry in this picture. One week later, he dropped dead in one of the small towns to which he had gone to teach. He had fallen asleep at the kitchen table, as usual, with his head in the Talmud. The next morning, when they tried to shake him awake, they discovered he was dead. There are two theories in the family as to the meaning of this event. Some people say, You see! He never should have had his picture taken. Others say, Thank God he had his picture taken before it was too late.

I seem to have inherited a deep distrust of photography from my great-grandfather. What few pictures there are of our family life have all been taken by my wife. I prefer memory. Memory has a much richer palette. It is more subjective and therefore more reliable. It doesn't pretend to be a mirror of objective truth. When my larger family gathers, we often watch a videotape of my father's last days. It was taken at one of my niece's birthday parties. I hate to watch it. The pale, emaciated ghost of a man who appears in that video is not my father. My memory of my father captures the fullness of who he was much more accurately.

Still, there may be more going on here than I realize. We had a videotape made of my daughter Hannah's Bat Mitzvah, and I hate to watch that one too, but for other reasons. That video forces me to look at myself. I like to think of myself as a mellow, laidback kind of father. But what I see when I look at myself in this video is a nervous, passive-aggressive fellow with a big phony smile on his face. So maybe there's another reason I don't like to look at these videos. Maybe I don't want to look at a moment-by-moment unfolding of the way I really am.

There is a story about a rabbi who was invited to a congregant's home to view the first showing of the videotape of the wedding he had recently performed for this man's daughter. As the tape begins, the rabbi and the cantor are seen standing alone under the wedding canopy blissfully unaware that the videotape is running. They can be heard making fun of both families and how poorly they are adapting to their new status as in-laws. Then the cantor makes a disparaging remark about the bride's mother's dress. He calls it a hideous *shmatte* (rag). Then the rabbi himself can be heard uttering a profane assessment of the groom's uncle.

The recording of serious misdeeds on tape, either video or audio, has become a commonplace of contemporary culture. We watched the Los Angeles police whaling on Rodney King, and Marion Berry, the mayor of Washington, D.C., buying crack in a cheap motel. It wasn't so common some thirty years ago, when White House aide Alexander Butterfield revealed the existence of a taping system in the Nixon Oval Office. The Watergate scandal was at its height, and for liberal Americans, this was the fulfillment of a deep fantasy. The whole world saw this president as he really was and not as he pretended to be. But it was also much more than that. It was the reenforcement of a deeply held intuitive belief: that all our actions are being recorded somewhere, that every move we make is being watched by someone.

Your days are like scrolls, Rabbi Bachya Ibn Pakuda wrote. Write on them only what you would like to have remembered. And at the very end of the Torah we find these ringing words: "Lend an ear, O Heaven, and I will speak. Listen, Earth, to the words of my mouth." The universe is watching us, the Torah suggests. The universe is witnessing what we do. And all of it is recorded. It is recorded on earth and it is recorded in the heavens as well.

—

This is also the suggestion of the great rabbinic legend that forms the cornerstone of our Rosh Hashanah observances, the story of Rabbi Crespudai and his three books, the Book of Death for the wholly evil, the Book of Life for the wholly righteous, and a third book for everyone in between.

The image of the three books calls us to look at our lives as if every deed, every word were being strictly recorded. If we really understood this, how differently might we have behaved? The rabbi and the cantor wouldn't have made their cutting wisecracks, the cops wouldn't have beaten up Rodney King, Marion Barry wouldn't have smoked crack, and Richard Nixon would have behaved like a mensch.

We keep trying to pose for the snapshot of our life, but at Rosh Hashanah our deepest need is to see the tape. And there really is such a tape. In fact there is a whole set of tapes. There is the Book of the World. There is the Book of the Body, the Book of Life, and the Book of the Heart.

So let's roll the videotape. First let's look at the Book of the World. Our collective unconscious is scrawled all over the world around us like graffiti. Look at the world. Here in San Francisco, look downtown at the glittering new skyline, the beautiful museums in Yerba Buena Gardens, the new ballpark at China Basin, the newly restored City Hall literally made of gold — a dream palace where people now stage fantasy weddings — and all of it surrounded by spanking new high-rise apartments and fancy hotels. Look at the street my synagogue is on. Every house on this street sells for a million dollars. One million dollars apiece. What does this book tell us? It tells us that we are extremely wealthy, even the most ordinary among us. This may very well be the high point of human history in terms of the number of people who have managed to accumulate significant wealth, or even in terms of the wealth enjoyed by people close to the middle of our economic culture. The stock market goes up, the stock market goes down, but regardless, most of us drive cars that are more luxurious than the houses our grandparents lived in. But let's look at this tape a little more closely. Let's look at the streets underneath these magnificent hotels. There are people sleeping there, there are children sleeping there, more and more every night, thousands of children sleeping on the streets of the city amid the wealth and the glitter.

Even when the stock market is down, we are incredibly wealthy as a nation. But as wealth increases exponentially in this society, so do poverty and homelessness, both in terms of numbers and in terms of the kinds of people who are afflicted by them. Now we have the working poor — people with full-time jobs who can't support their families. Fully one-third of the workforce is in this category now. And we have suburban poor, and most heartbreaking of all, poor children — a growing legion of them. Housing costs are skyrocketing all over the country, but we have cut the safety net to shreds. We've cut welfare to the bone. We've cut the few meager housing subsidies we used to provide. We have made the balanced budget into an idol — a god that must be worshipped at all costs, the Moloch to whom we sacrifice our young. Rabbi Elliot Dorf, one of the leading contemporary scholars of Jewish law, has written that while a balanced budget is a perfectly legitimate social goal, it is totally irrelevant where social welfare is concerned, at least according to Jewish law. By Jewish law, the only thing that may be considered when helping the poor is the need of the poor. We are not allowed to say, We will not care for the poor because the budget won't be balanced if we do.

Judaism came into a primitive world where the poor were demonized. Poverty was seen as the consequence of a moral fault. The poor didn't deserve to be helped. But Judaism came to say that this is not how heaven sees things. Heaven thinks that the poor are to be helped, not blamed. But the primitive impulse to blame the poor for their plight persists. Just look at the evidence of the videotape. Look out at the streets. The homeless, in particular, have been singled out for this kind of demonization. They're all drug addicts, the thinking goes. They're all mentally ill, so let's just get rid of them, let's just run them out of town. It's true. You can look at the tape. There are a lot of drug addicts, there are a lot of mentally ill out there — we've been closing public drug treatment and mental health clinics for years. But let's look at the tape a little more carefully. Let's look at who is really out there. The fastest-growing group out on the streets is children, and the truth is that families — working families — are increasingly finding them-selves having to choose between paying rent and putting food on the table. The working poor can no longer afford both. This is what we see when we take a close look at the videotape, at the Book of the World. We see greed and gluttony, and we see neglect, and we see a growing army of innocent sufferers, whose cries fall on deaf ears down here but are heard and recorded in heaven.

Let's roll another tape. Let's look at the Book of the Body. I once knew a prosperous and successful architect who had raised a family in a beautiful home in a comfortable suburb of San Fran-cisco. But when his two children became teenagers, they got involved with drugs. His son and his daughter were both, in fact, seriously addicted to drugs. At first he was furious with them. How could they ruin his perfect life this way, especially after all he had done for them, after all he had given them? But then he got involved with their rehab, with family therapy, and so on. One day in the middle of a therapy session, his daughter got up and started screaming at him. You've never been there for us, she said. Not for one minute. What are you talking about? he said. I've provided you with everything you could have possibly wanted. I gave you clothing. I gave you a beautiful home. I sent you to the best schools. But you never gave us yourself, his daughter said. Not once. Not for one minute.

This man was struck to the core of his being by what his daughter said, because he knew immediately that it was absolutely true. So being a fairly scrupulous and thorough person, he set about trying to discover why it was he had withheld himself from his children so thoroughly that they had both grown up seeking love from the end of a hypodermic needle. He went into therapy, and that didn't work. He did encounter groups, and that didn't work either. Then he started working with a Reichian therapist, someone who worked directly with the body, and this person focused with him on a particular knot of musculature in his back for many months, and one day he just felt this muscle letting go, unclenching for the first time in his memory. The very next moment, he felt a mind-numbing fear, a total, all-embracing, paralyzing fear. The moment after that, he had the strangest sensation. He certainly felt this fear. He had rarely been so certain of any feeling in his life. But he was equally certain that he wasn't afraid of anything. He was surrounded by fear, but he wasn't afraid. Finally he realized what he was feeling. The fear that had

—

surrounded him, that had paralyzed him, that had stood between him and everyone he had ever attempted to love, was his mother's fear. He wasn't afraid, but his mother was. His mother had been an extremely anxious woman, and when he was a child he had assimilated her fear; he had taken it into his own body. And this fear had been lodged there ever since. It had been a constant barrier. It had affected every relationship he had ever had. It had caused him to withhold love, to keep himself apart from the people he cared about, to distance himself from everyone and everything in a thousand unconscious ways. Now he could see it. Now he could read the Book of the Body. The truth of our lives is the closest thing to us there is, as the Torah reminds us. It is right in front of our eyes. It is embedded in our bodies.

There are several volumes entitled the Book of Life on our shelf, but we want to be sure we pull down the one that will be useful to us. Reading the Book of Our Successes, the book of the way we have presented ourselves to the world, the book of the prizes, the family car, the six-figure income, the trophy spouse — this book will tell us nothing we don't already know. After all, we wrote this book. This is the book we spent our life energy writing so that people would think highly of us, which is to say, so that they would fear us and envy us. This isn't the book we need to read. This isn't the tape we need to watch. We need to watch the tape that has painstakingly recorded everything, including our failures, our dysfunctions, and our heartbreak. We have to look at this tape long enough to see the recurring patterns. What keeps coming back? What circumstances keep repeating themselves in our lives? Why do we keep losing jobs? Why do we keep losing husbands? Why do we keep getting into the same kinds of conflicts with people wherever we go?

—

Our families record our real lives with an unflinching precision. This is a tape that never stops rolling. We may look lovely in that snapshot, that picture of kindliness and good cheer we present to the world at large, but when we come home and take out our frustrations on our wives and children, the tape is still running. Our behavior is stored forever in our children's hearts. A good question to ask ourselves as we plunge into the process of Teshuvah on Rosh Hashanah is this: What would we read about ourselves if our own children wrote a book about who we were? How does our family see us? What would the tape reveal when our guard was down?

And we can be sure of this too: all those peripheral moments, those moments we thought no one would notice, they'll be on the tape too. The tape didn't stop running in between the events we imagined were important. It caught all those small, in-between moments too, the moments when we thought no one was watching. It counts, even if we felt invisible when we were doing it. And every once in a while, that motorist to whom we have just given the finger, or that woman whom we have just ogled, catches our eye, and we freeze. We see ourselves in their gaze, our rage and our lust. We probably don't like what we see in those moments, but they have a kind of power nevertheless. They remind us that we are being watched. We can see ourselves in the eyes of these strangers.

And the tape is rolling when we deal with people we feel are invisible — witnesses, toll booth collectors, indigent strangers who ask us for handouts on the street. Our interactions with people whom we might be tempted to regard as unimportant tell a great deal about who we are. At my synagogue, I am often shocked to discover that people who always speak to me with unfailing

consideration and the utmost respect regularly berate the synagogue secretaries mercilessly when they call for appointments or
for better seating arrangements for the High Holidays. I think
they must imagine that since I am God's agent on earth, God only
pays attention to their interactions with me and doesn't register
their conversations with the secretaries. Why, after all, would God
be interested in unimportant people like my secretaries? But the
annoying thing about God is that God seems to be interested in
everyone. It's on the tape. It's written in the book of our life.

And after the Book of the World and the Book of the Body,
the truth of our life is also written in the Book of the Heart. We
can feel it there, pressing up against our rib cage. It is perfectly
self-evident. All we have to do is read it. If we just stop and quiet
ourselves, our broken hearts announce themselves. We know our
disappointment very well. We know our shame and our failure.
During the Days of Awe, we pound our heart repeatedly as we
recite the Vidui, the confessional prayer that is repeated over and
over again in the High Holiday liturgy. We point at the heart. We
pound at the heart until it opens and we can read it.

Why does it take such an effort? Largely, I think, because we
don't feel safe about exposing our hearts. We are used to being on
the defensive — to having people use our heartbreak and failure
against us. This is one of the reasons the twelve-step programs
have become one of the most successful American spiritual movements. They provide people with a safe place to read the book of
their own heartbreak. And they begin by acknowledging that they
can't read it, they can't see it, without the help of heaven.

An event that taught me a great deal about how we Americans feel about heartbreak was a PBS series that ran in the seven-

ties called *An American Family*. This was perhaps the first conspic-
uous example of public exposure by videotape. This show docu-
mented the life of the Loud family of Santa Barbara, California. It
focused an unforgiving lens on every moment in the life of this
family for a period of seven months, and during that time, the family completely fell apart. It was a classic illustration of Heisenberg's
Uncertainty Principle — that the act of observation changes what
is being observed. Later, people asked the Louds why they had permitted this devastating intrusion on their private lives. They said
they were proud of their family. They had a great marriage. They
were successful. They had a beautiful house, and it was full of attractive kids. They thought it would be great to show themselves to the
world. But as they lived their lives under the camera's unflinching
gaze, the family became conscious of themselves, and they didn't
particularly like what they saw. The camera exposed a life of deceit,
adultery, cruelty, drug abuse, and homosexuality, which back then
was still regarded as a matter of shame. The husband was a terrible
philanderer, as it happened. The daughter was addicted to speed.
The older son was a homosexual who came out of the closet as the
series was being filmed. Before the show was over, the Louds were
divorced and at least one of their children had run away from
home. And how did America receive all this? The Louds became
an object of disdain and derision. People wrote letters to their
newspapers and called in to talk shows. What a terrible family, they
said. Why are we looking at their lives? What does this have to do
with us? They continued to watch, of course, but despising the
Louds became a national pastime.

I will never forget the moment Pat Loud, the mother of the
family, finally got it. It happened somewhere around the seventh

or eighth episode. She finally saw her family, she saw her life, as it really was on this video that never stopped running, this book of her real life, and it completely broke her heart. Her husband was unfaithful. Her children were in terrible trouble. The photograph for which she had so carefully posed was crumbling to dust, and her heart was breaking. The minute it finally did, I fell hopelessly in love with her. All the way from the other side of the TV screen, I was smitten. That's how I always feel when I see someone in the full reality of their suffering, when I see them with their hearts broken open. I've never seen a human being in that condition who wasn't exquisitely beautiful. I was amazed to discover that most people didn't see her that way. Most people thought she was a dope.

But I am sure that God did not. God also fell in love with Pat Loud, of that I am quite certain. This is what God always does when God reads the Book of the Heart. This is how God is different from Big Brother, who also knows everything we do and say, but who uses it against us. God watches the whole video with a boundless, heartbreaking compassion.

This is the God of the classical Midrash, in any case, a God who watches us stumble and blunder through this world, weeping profusely as He does. So it is with the destruction of the Great Temple of Jerusalem. God watches the whole tape: the people of Israel sinning egregiously, the people of Israel engaging in gratuitous hatred, first the Babylonians and then the Romans marching on Jerusalem, and then the Temple finally falling. And when it does, God weeps.

And God wept at the death of Moses. Talk about heartbreak! Let's roll the videotape of Moses' life. When we think of Moses, we tend to see Charlton Heston. The Great Law-Giver.

The greatest of all the Prophets. The deliverer of his people. But Rabbi David Wolpe offers the following synopsis of Moses' actual life. The first time we see Moses as an adult, he walks out of his father's palace and murders a man. Then he runs away, marries a Midianite, and lives in exile among strangers. God selects Moses for the great mission of delivering his people, but what does Moses say? No thank you. I don't speak well. No one will believe me, and so on. But God says, Look, you have no choice in the matter. I'll give you good allies — your brother, your sister, and the people Israel. So Moses sets out on this mission with all these allies, and one by one they betray him. His sister Miriam betrays him. She slanders him for marrying an Ethiopian, and he has to pray to God to save her life. Then his brother Aaron betrays him. When Moses is up in heaven receiving the Torah, the greatest moment of his life, Aaron is helping the Children of Israel build the golden calf. And the people betray him too. In fact they betray him right and left. This seems to be what they do for a living in the wilderness; they betray Moses. They refuse to go into the land when they are supposed to, they rebel against him and accuse him of arrogating power to himself, they complain incessantly about the food and the water.

Finally God and Moses are alone together, just the two of them coursing through the desert. When they come to the edge of the Promised Land, what does God say? God says, You die here. Why? Because I once told you to speak to a rock and you hit it instead. Big deal! Forget all the Midrash — Moses was a leader, he was held to a higher standard of responsibility, yada, yada, yada. Just look at the tape. He was a human being. He made a little mistake. Is that any reason to deprive him of the fruition of a lifetime mission that he had never asked for in the first place? Finally we see Moses begging for his life, pitifully calling upon heaven and earth and the Torah to intercede on his behalf for one more hour, one more day. And what does God do then? God listens. God says, Moses, you are a human being, and all human beings have to die, and now is your time. But I'll attend to you. I'll bury you myself. I'll give you my full attention. And then God comes down and takes Moses' soul with a kiss, weeping, weeping, weeping as He does.

God saw Moses' bare, broken heart, and God fell in love with Moses, the same way I fell in love with Pat Loud.

At Rosh Hashanah we begin to acknowledge the truth of our lives. This truth is written wherever we look. It is written on the streets of our city; it is written in our bodies; it is written in our lives and in our hearts. We have a deep need to know this truth — our lives quite literally depend on it. But we can't seem to get outside ourselves long enough to see it. And besides, we are terrified of the truth.

But this is a needless terror.

What is there is already so. It's on the tape. Owning up to it doesn't make it worse. Not being open about it doesn't make it go away. And we know we can stand the truth. It is already here and we are already enduring it.

And the tape is rolling. The hand is writing. Someone is watching us endure it, waiting to heal us the moment we awake and watch along.

From the great pit of our heart, we sense the seeing eye, we sense the knowing ear, watching the drama of our lives unfold, watching with unbearable compassion.

—

CHAPTER SEVEN

What the Soul

Does While the

Gates Are Still Open

The Ten Days of Teshuvah

For ten days, the gates are open and the world is fluid. We are finally awake, if only in fits and starts, if only to toss and turn. For ten days, transformation is within our grasp. For ten days, we can imagine ourselves not as fixed and immutable beings, but rather as a limitless field upon which qualities and impulses rise up and fall away again like waves on the sea. Some of these impulses rise up with particular intensity. We may even experience them as afflictions, but they can be the keys to our transformation. Their intensity points to the disequilibrium and dysfunction in us that is in need of transformation.

For ten days, the field of mind is like a painting by Kandinsky. Energy and form float in that field, and we have the sense that we can shape our lives by choosing where to invest our focus and intention, by choosing which forms to follow and which to let go.

This is not a linear process, not something that takes a clear nor even discernible path. Rather it happens in fits and starts. Sometimes it may not even seem to be happening at all. But the gates are in fact open, and if our intention is aligned with this spiritual reality, then transformation also opens as a real possibility, even if it doesn't manifest itself right away.

Parshat Netzavim is the beginning of the grand coda of the Torah. It is usually read the week before Rosh Hashanah, and since no new readings are introduced until after the holiday, Netzavim hangs over the Ten Days of Teshuvah like a ghostly presence. This is fortunate, as it happens, because Parshat Netzavim addresses Teshuvah itself, the process of active transformation we experience during the ten days, more directly and to greater effect than any other portion of the Torah.

> And it shall come to pass when all these things have come
>   upon you,
> The blessings and the curses that I have set before you,
> And they will rise up again [*ha-shev-ota*] in your heart
> Among the nations to whom the Lord your God has
>   driven you
> And you will return [*v-shav-ta*] to the Lord your God
>   and listen to God's voice. . . .
> Then the Lord your God will turn [*v-shav*] your captivity
> And have compassion on you and turn [*v-shav*]

—

And gather you in from all the nations where you have been
scattered. . . .
And God will circumcise the foreskin of your heart
So that you can love God with all your heart and with all
your soul. . . .
And you will turn [*ta-shuv*] and you will hear the voice of
God
And do all the commandments which I have commanded
you this day. . . .
And God will turn [*ya-shuv*] and rejoice over you again for
the good,
The way God rejoiced over your ancestors. . . .
If you turn [*ta-shuv*] to the Lord your God with all your
heart and with all your soul. . . .

DEUTERONOMY 30:1–10

The most apparent aspect of this passage is that the word-
root *shuv* (to turn, to return, to repent — the root of the word
Teshuvah) is repeated seven times. As we have noted, this sort of
ritual repetition signifies that the word is extremely significant.
Here it illuminates several important facets of the process of
Teshuvah.

First of all, we learn that Teshuvah can arise in the most
hopeless circumstances. In fact it often seems to begin that way.
This passage begins in the darkest days of exile, when we are sitting "among the nations to whom the Lord your God has driven
you." Most of us only embark on the difficult and wrenching path
of transformation when we feel we have no choice but to do so,

when we feel as if our backs are to the wall, when the circumstances of our lives have pushed us to the point of a significant leave-taking, when we have suffered loss or death, divorce or unemployment. Transformation is just too hard for us to volunteer for. Interestingly, God is depicted as the one who is doing the pushing here. We are in the predicament that has brought us to the point of transformation because God has driven us there. In other words, that predicament is part of the process. It is a gift, the agent of our turning.

Second, this passage shows us the complexity of transformation. Transformation is not something that happens once and for all time. The people turn three different times in this passage, and as it closes, they are promised a great blessing, but only if they continue to turn in the future.

Transformation does not have a beginning, a middle, or an end. We never reach the end of Teshuvah. It is always going on. We are awake for a moment, and then we are asleep again. Teshuvah seems to proceed in a circular motion. Every step away is also a step toward home.

And it may never be clear to us that the work of transformation has borne fruit. This is usually the case in the realm of spiritual practice. Real spiritual transformation invariably takes a long time to manifest itself in our lives. Spectacular, immediate results — sudden changes in aspect or in the way we see the world — are always suspect, and usually suggest a superficial rather than a profound transformation. Profound transformation only manifests itself over time. When Jacob has his great vision of the ladder and realizes he has been visited by God, he exclaims out loud, "My God! God has been in this place all along and I never knew it!" From this moment of epiphany, we expect he will be changed. We are disappointed when he continues to behave like the same manipulative schmo he has always been. But when we look at the larger arc of Jacob's life, we see that this vision really does effect a profound change in him. It's just that this change isn't evident right away. It takes more than twenty years for it to take root.

My older daughter, Hannah, had a famously difficult passage through adolescence, in the course of which she dropped out of school, crashed all our attempts to discipline her, and lived in a state of open warfare with us. Out of desperation, we enrolled her in Urban Pioneers, a program of nonacademic learning that focused on an intense exposure to the wilderness. The kids in this program, many of them with histories similar to hers, took rigorous training in climbing, rappelling, and other wilderness skills, and then went out for an extended exploration of the High Sierras. On the last day of this trip, the kids were split up into small groups and sent out on their own without guides or counselors. It was supposed to be an exercise in self-reliance, but on the day in question, a fierce and sudden storm overcame the Sierras and Hannah's group became lost. For four days they staggered through the mountains, pelted by high winds, rain, and snow, running out of food and water, soaked to the bone. Several of them came down with hypothermia. Hannah kept one of these kids alive by lying on top of her and warming her with the heat of her body for an entire night. The kids all came to believe that they were doomed. Certainly Hannah believed this. But a helicopter spotted them on the fourth day, and when Hannah came home, she was positively radiant. There was a glow in her face as she told

—

us what had happened. When she believed she was going to die, she had a great illumination. She realized how much she loved us and how bad she felt about the way our relationship had been going in recent years. She felt bad about the way her life was going too. But everything would be different now. She had seen the light. She was going to change.

She came home on a Friday. By Sunday it was quite clear that everything was depressingly the same. She stayed out all night on Saturday, and on Sunday we had another terrible fight. My wife and I shrugged our shoulders. So much for everything being different, we said. But six months later, it was quite clear that everything *was* different, and that the change could be clearly traced to her near-death experience in the Sierras.

So the process of Teshuvah is neither clear nor linear. And who is the principal actor in all this? Is it us or is it God? In the passage from Netzavim, sometimes we are the subject of the turning, and sometimes God is the subject, all of which seems to suggest that Teshuvah — transformation — is a reciprocal process that depends on both God and us. No one else can do transformation for us, but on the other hand we can't do it by ourselves either. The possibility of transformation always exists, but we have to consciously turn toward it in order to activate it. At the same time, our initiative can only take us so far. After that, we have to have faith. We have to depend on the universe to support the flowering of our intention.

So the first ten verses of Deuteronomy 30 give us a very accurate picture of this process of transformation, its complexity, its interactive quality, its confusing, nonlinear course. But the next four verses give us some extraordinarily direct and clear advice about precisely how to do Teshuvah, how to effect our own transformation.

> Because this commandment [to do Teshuvah] is not too wonderful for you and is not distant from you either.
> It is not in heaven, so you can't say, "Who can go up to heaven and bring it to us and cause us to hear it so that we can do it?"
> And it is not beyond the sea, so you can't say, "Who can go across the sea and bring it to us and cause us to hear it so that we can do it?"
> But the word is very near to you, in your mouth and in your heart, so you can do it.
>
> DEUTERONOMY 30:11–14

Teshuvah begins with a turn, a turn away from the external world and toward the inner realm of the heart. We effect this turn in many ways. If we are not used to solitude or contemplation, if we are normally consumed by a frantic round of activity, if we live our lives at a rapid pace, then simply stopping — simply coming to synagogue every day and praying, setting aside a small period of time each day for contemplation, observing the Sabbath or some other conscious retreat from the world of activity and stress — can suddenly leave us in confrontation with the contents of our heart. These contents are an open secret. We already know this secret. Often all that's required of us is to be still for a moment, and the heart begins to disclose itself to us of its own accord.

But the heart is a mysterious and complex thing. The irony is, if we are experienced at prayer or meditation, if we already

—

157

observe a regular period of retreat from the frenetic rush of worldly activity, we might find the heart more difficult to find. We might already have some familiarity with the feelings and impulses that are sitting on the surface of our heart, and we might need a more concerted effort to get beneath that. In the chapter on Elul, we reviewed the role prayer and meditation play in this process. Both of these activities sneak up on the heart. They disarm the heart by focusing on something else — the breath or the body or the words of the prayer book — and then the heart, which has always craved our attention anyway, unwittingly discloses itself by stealing our attention away from our breathing or our prayers with a continuous stream of thoughts and feelings and impulses.

But why does the heart require such an indirect approach? Why won't it just open wide when we ask it to? Why does it resist us so? We are sentimental about the heart, but the truth is, most of us spend a great deal of time and energy avoiding the heart at all costs. Really, we are afraid of what we might find there. We don't even know where it is or how we might find it, but somehow we understand there is a lot of pain there. If we are human, we suffer. The heart holds our suffering. The pain we most need to deal with is sitting right there on our hearts in plain sight, or else it is just inside its dark chambers.

In either case we are not inclined to look at it. We live in a culture that conditions us to avoid suffering, and the consequence of this is that we live at some distance from our heart. We are not in the habit of looking at it, but of distracting ourselves from its content. As we begin the process of Teshuvah, we need to make a conscious effort to overcome the momentum of this denial and avoidance. This is an effort well worth making. That pain, that afflictive energy that rests on the surface of our hearts and just below it as well, will be the catalyst for our transformation. The nature of our pain points us to the nature of the transformation we need to make. If we are angry, we need to move toward inhabiting our anger and then letting go of it. If we are in despair, we need to move toward hope. But the intensity of our pain is even more helpful in this process than its particular cast. As we sit in the boundless field of mind during the ten days of transformation, impulses and feelings rise up and fall away all around us. Those impulses and feelings that assert themselves with particular force are the ones we are most likely to follow. This is the great gift of suffering. Intense afflictive states — anger, boredom, fear, guilt, impatience, grief, disappointment, dejection, anxiety, despair — are the great markers of our Teshuvah. By their very intensity, they call us to transformation.

These feelings are so familiar to us we usually believe them to be part of our intrinsic being. They are not, and in this sacred time of transformation, while the gates of heaven are open and we are finally awake, we can see that they are not. We can see that they are just impulses, arising for a moment, the way wind and rain and snow arise for a moment in the world. They are wind and rain and snow, but they are not the world. They are not us. They only become us by our own choice, by our choosing to see them that way, by our choosing to cling to them so tenaciously. We can make another choice if we wish to. We can choose to allow these feelings to rise up and then let them fall away again like a hot breeze.

And this is the simplest and most frightening truth about all this business. Anger is a choice. Boredom is a choice. Fear is a choice. No one can hold a gun to our heads in this regard. No one can make us feel this feeling. No one can crawl inside us and alter us. We are responsible for the state of our own consciousness.

The great drama of this season is the drama of choice. The power of choice is immense. We can choose to let go of anger, boredom, fear, guilt, impatience, grief, disappointment, dejection, anxiety, and despair, and we can make this choice moment by moment, and we can make this choice in a broader way as well. We can let go of each constituent feeling as we become aware of it, and we can form a clear and continuous intention to let these feelings go.

When we recite the great formula of Rebbe Nachman, for example — If anyone has hurt or harmed me, knowingly or unknowingly, I forgive them — we are planting the seeds of forgiveness and love. We are awakening the powerful force of intention in our minds, and even if it doesn't bear fruit right away — even if we don't feel a great rush of love at first — we can trust the laws of nature and the power of intention to support the flowering of forgiveness in our souls and in the world. We form our intention and then we let heaven and earth bear witness. Opening to forgiveness, we begin to see it all around us.

❄

The Ten Days of Teshuvah are days of renewal, days when we are not only concerned with change and transformation, but also with reinvigorating, refreshing, and reimagining our lives, days when we are obliged to ask ourselves a number of difficult and unpleasant questions.

What do we do when we run out of gas? What do we do when we feel like we're running on empty?

What do we do when everything we do seems dull, when life seems barren and drained of color and taste, when the landscape that used to thrill us with its beauty now lies before us flat and dull, its radiance drained away?

What do we do when we can't summon the enthusiasm we used to have for our work or for our marriage or even for a simple walk through the world?

What do we do when we admit to ourselves, in the secret darkness of our heart, that we really don't care anymore about the things we used to care about? Here we are in the life or the job or the marriage that we got ourselves into when we did care; here we are, daily required to espouse feelings and principles and justifications we once fervently believed, but which we now neither feel nor believe anymore. What do we do when we are daily afflicted with a sense of having sold out, of going through the motions, of doing something we don't really believe in?

What do we do when we realize we are suffering from that contemporary epidemic, the burnout syndrome?

What do we do when our life becomes characterized by a sense of meaninglessness, by a loss of passion, by fatigue and depression?

What do we do, that is, besides divorce our spouses, drink ourselves into oblivion, drug ourselves insensate, drown ourselves in shopping or television or sports, or try to simulate passion with gambling, pornography, or illicit sex?

And what do we do when our religious life begins to feel this way, when the first intoxication with Shabbat begins to pale, when we no longer feel that extra wave of spirituality descending on us at the onset of Shabbat as we used to?

What happens when the prayer service no longer brings us into a sense of communion with God? What happens when the words of the prayer service no longer mean anything to us, no longer connect us with the long continuity of Jewish spirituality, but instead begin to grate? What happens when we become so tired of them we can't bear to hear them anymore? What happens when they just seem to drone on and on?

What happens when meditation ceases to be a daily entry into a deeper state of consciousness and becomes an endless reiteration of the most puerile and mundane thoughts imaginable?

The great Zen teacher Shunryu Suzuki wrote:

It is hard to keep our mind pure and our practice pure. . . . The goal of practice is always to keep our beginner's mind. Suppose you recite [a prayer] only once. It might be a very good recitation. But what would happen to you if you recited it twice, three times, four times, or more? You might easily lose your original attitude towards it. The same thing will happen in your other . . . practices. For a while you will keep your beginner's mind, but if you continue to practice one, two, three years or more, although you may improve some, you are liable to lose the limitless meaning of original mind.

God renews the entire world every day. We make this declaration every day in our prayer service, acknowledging that every day can be a newly experienced birth and that we can once again see the world with the newness of a child. And we also thank God every day for the miracles that are constantly with us, evening, morning, and afternoon. But how do we attune ourselves to this miracle when all we feel is dull and stale? How do we recapture our sense of what the eminent scholar and theologian Abraham Joshua Heschel called "wonder" or "radical amazement"? How do we recapture a sense of poetry, joy, and surprise in what now seems old and stale? How do we avoid routinization?

In the Midrash Sifre on Deuteronomy we read:

Take to heart these words that I charge you today — *Hayom* — Today — these words are not to be in your sight like some old ordinance, to which no one is paying attention any longer, but they are to be in your sight like a new ordinance toward which everyone is running.

Or in the words of the scholar and philosopher Martin Buber:

When we do not believe that God renews the work of creation every day, then our religious practice becomes old and routine and boring. As it says in the Psalms, "Do not cast me off when I am old." That is, do not let my world become old.

Or in the words of Abraham Joshua Heschel:

As civilization advances, the sense of wonder declines. Such decline is an alarming symptom of our state of mind. Mankind will not perish for want of information, but only for want of appreciation. The beginning of our happiness lies in the understanding that life without wonder is not worth living. What we lack is not a will to believe, but a will to wonder.

—

Heschel is warning us. This is not a mere theological problem; it is a matter of life and death. There are people who die from burnout and from the spiritual and emotional deadening that comes in its wake. I have seen such people with my own eyes. They have strokes. They have heart attacks. I have sat by the sides of their beds. Sometimes they actually die from these things and sometimes they live on but in a deep state of depression, a living death, but a death nonetheless. There are people who are dead even when alive. Rashi, the great medieval Torah commentator, suggests that when we read in the Book of Deuteronomy, "I have put before you this day life and death, a blessing and a curse, therefore choose life," the verse is talking about spiritual life and spiritual death. The blessing is refreshment — the renewal of the soul. The curse is boredom, staleness, frustration, failure.

But what can we do when we find ourselves spiritually dead while still breathing? How do we transform this curse into its corresponding blessing?

Our first inclination is often to change the external circumstances of our life — to change our physical environment. Don't just stand there, we tell ourselves. Do something. Do anything. This is actually a solution Jewish tradition sometimes suggests as well. "Change your place, change your luck," the Talmud tells us. Perhaps if we make a major life change, if we actually move to another city or another state, our luck will change as well.

The conventional wisdom these days is that you can change your situation but your problems will continue to pursue you. And while this is often true, sometimes the situation *is* the problem. Sometimes we just have the wrong job. Sometimes we are just stuck in a bad relationship. In such cases, "Change your place, change your luck" can be good advice.

Most of the time, however, the conventional wisdom is correct. We can change our lives around completely — change careers, divorce our husbands, move to another city — and this feeling of deadness might even go away for a while. But far more often than not, it will return, and return with a vengeance; far more often, the problem is within and not without.

This, the psychologists tell us, is why there are so many suicides on the Golden Gate Bridge. San Francisco is a place many people come to out of a belief in "change your place, change your luck." It is a place many come to because they believe their problem is that they live in Fairlawn, New Jersey. So they move someplace else, and then they move someplace else again, and then finally they end up in San Francisco, the most beautiful city in the world. And after a very brief while, all the unhappiness they felt in Fairlawn, New Jersey, returns, and they feel desperate. But here the land ends. There is nowhere else to go. They feel as if they have cashed in their last option. As the writer and meditation teacher Jon Kabat-Zinn reminds us, wherever we go, there we are. So moving ourselves to someplace else rarely solves anything.

Sometimes, however, a simple change in routine might really suffice to set off the kind of inner change this problem demands. Heschel writes that the greatest hindrance to awareness of the divine is our adjustment to conventional notions and mental clichés. Wonder, or radical amazement, he suggests, is a state of maladjustment to words and notions. Moshe Cordovero, the great medieval Kabalist, also recommends a kind of intentional maladjustment as a strategy for returning to God. "It is a good idea to make some sort of alteration in your food and drink and in your clothing," he writes. "For example, one week do not eat fruit; another week, do not eat meat or drink wine, or do not eat hot food."

I had a friend once who had divorced her husband. They had shared a great house together, and she had gotten the house in the divorce settlement, but now she faced a terrible problem. She loved the house, but how could she stay in it without being constantly reminded of the marriage? Finally she hit upon a solution. She changed all the furniture in the house around. She changed the orientation of every room. Furniture that used to face north and south now faced east and west and vice versa. It worked perfectly. She stayed in the house, but she felt as if she had a new life in it.

Spiritual deadness is a habit. Something in us wants to be dead — wants to escape our reality — and we've expressed this desire in a hundred little patterns and habits. So a physical shaking up of our stale routines might actually serve to loosen us up inside and lead the way to inner change.

David Roskies, a professor of Jewish literature at the Jewish Theological Seminary, speaks frequently of the need to defamiliarize the liturgy, to set old words in new melodies, and old melodies in new words. Marcia Falk, whose *Book of Blessings* offers us a radical retranslation of traditional liturgy, shakes up the classical liturgy so thoroughly that cracks appear in our apprehension of it, and more than once I have found God coming in through these cracks.

But we can only change our external routines so many times before this remedy stops working too. When I was being interviewed at rabbinical school, one of my interrogators asked me why

I had written G–d instead of God in my admissions essays. I told him that I didn't want to get habituated to the word God. I didn't want to speak of God without really thinking of or experiencing God. So I used a hyphen to remind me that that word is not the same thing as God. Well, what happens when you get habituated to G–d? he asked me. Well, then I guess I'll go to an asterisk, I replied.

But his point was well taken; eventually the asterisk stops working too, and sooner or later we have to address the inner roots of the problem of burnout and routinization directly.

Fortunately for us, our tradition has many useful suggestions as to how we might do this. "You should turn your mind toward God before you pray, before you study Torah and before you eat," says Rabbi Moshe Teitlebaum. Turn your mind toward God; this sounds like a simple, even a self-evident, proposition, but it's an essential first step in the process of spiritual renewal.

The first thing we should do when we feel we have lost all our passion is to try to find it. This involves a kind of inner turning, an expression of will, an expression of faith, the belief that like God, this passion exists even though we neither feel it nor see it at the moment.

There is a paradigm well mapped out in the novels of Hermann Hesse, especially *Siddhartha*. *Siddhartha* is the story of a young monk who is lured away from a long and extremely devoted spiritual path by his lust for a beautiful woman, a lust that alters the course of his life. He becomes a businessman, totally involved in the corruption and the pleasures of ordinary life. He marries, becomes dissolute, takes up gambling and adultery, and loses his wife. His son rebels against him and finally rejects him altogether, causing him unbearable pain. Finally, broken and despairing, he becomes a recluse, a ferryman, carrying people back and forth across the river. And there on the river, the deep and abiding wisdom he sought in his youth begins to ripen in his soul, until he finally comes to the following understanding:

> The world . . . is not imperfect or slowly evolving along a path to perfection. No, it is perfect at every moment. Every sin already carries grace within it, all small children are potential old men. All sucklings have death within them, all dying people — eternal life. . . . Everything is good. Everything is perfect, . . . death as well as life, sin as well as holiness, wisdom as well as folly. Everything is necessary. Everything needs only my agreement, my assent, my loving understanding, my turning toward.

The critical moment in this story is a subtle turn of mind — a moment when the hero must bring his consciousness back to the path he abandoned, back to the path he has imagined doesn't even exist anymore.

There are times in my own religious life when prayer brings me into a very strong and immediate sense of the presence of God. But then there are long dry spells when this doesn't happen, and I begin to doubt myself and to wonder if it ever happened at all, or if I simply imagined it. What usually brings me out of such a dry spell is a simple inner turn. I simply turn toward that inner place, that radiant nexus of mind, heart, and soul, where I used to feel the presence of God, and lo and behold, God is still there waiting for me. Renewal often begins when we turn toward this place even when it seems utterly distant. In our tradition, this turning often takes the form of prayer.

"If because of my sins, which are many and great, there is no angel to defend me, then do You Yourself see that a hole is dug under the wall of Your heavenly palace for me to squeeze through and come into Your presence." So reads Rabbenu Yonah's famous prayer of reconciliation with God, a prayer that we might squeeze into God's presence at those times when we feel squeezed out. And Rabbi David Lida, a Spanish Kabalist, said: "Accustom yourself to say again and again, 'Create for me, God, a pure heart and renew within me an upright heart.'"

Prayer creates space for this renewal. Prayer galvanizes our will. Prayer opens us to the possibility of change so that we notice when an opening arises, which we might not have noticed without being so prepared.

So step number one in the process of spiritual renewal, according to our tradition, is this kind of subtle inner turning either through prayer or through faith. Step number two is almost precisely the opposite. It involves neither turning nor any kind of movement at all. It involves being still.

When we defy the sense of meaninglessness that afflicts us, galvanize ourselves for transformation, and open ourselves to the possibility of change, we in no way deny or run away from the reality of our situation. In fact we do exactly the opposite; we embrace the emptiness. It is precisely our failure to inhabit our life which has rendered it dull and meaningless. So while we defy the meaninglessness of our life, the act of defiance consists in our refusal to run away and our resolve instead to fill it with our consciousness. We live it, and then we dare it to remain dull and meaningless.

One of Rebbe Nachman's most famous stories is about a prince who came to believe he was a turkey. He took off all his clothes and got under the table and lived there on scraps and crumbs and bones. The king called in many doctors, but none of them could cure him. Finally, he called in a certain wise man, who took off his own clothes and sat down under the table with him. I am a turkey, the prince told him. I am a turkey too, the wise man said. The two of them sat there together for a very long time, and then the wise man said, Do you think a turkey can't wear a shirt? You can wear a shirt and still be a turkey. So the prince put on a shirt. Do you think you can't be a turkey and wear trousers? So the prince put on his trousers too, and in this way the wise man coaxed the prince to put on all his clothes, to eat real food, and finally to come up from under the table and to sit at the table. In the end, the prince was completely cured.

Avraham Greenbaum, a contemporary interpreter of Rebbe Nachman's work, writes:

The wise man went under the table, and the very first thing he did, his first lesson, was just to sit there. You might have thought he would have been anxious to get started and take the first steps in his plan to cure the prince. In fact, sitting was the first step. Indeed, if you think about the story as a whole, you notice that most of the time the wise man took to cure the prince was spent just sitting with him. This is because the ability to sit calmly is one of the most important prerequisites of clear-headedness. The Hebrew term for a calm, settled state of mind — *yishuv ha-dat* — is bound up with the concept of sitting. *Daat* is awareness or consciousness, intellectual, emotional, meditative, intuitive or all of the above. The word *yishuv* is a noun from the Hebrew root *yashav*, meaning to sit, or to dwell or to inhabit.

The verb *yashav* also has a transitive form, *le-yashev*, which means to cause someone to sit or dwell, which in plain English would be to settle. *Yishuv hadaat* means to settle the mind. A *yishuv* is a settlement — a habitation, a place where people have set down a foundation and are making a stand or a sit. So sitting in this sense not only signifies the physical act of seating the body quietly. It also suggests the whole principle of taking a break from the activities of day to day living in order to fully inhabit our lives. The Hebrew word for sitting is thus connected with the idea of Shabbat, when we pause and sit back from our workaday activities in order to cultivate the spirit, to inhabit our lives with spirit and consciousness.

A certain rebbe had a close disciple who fell into a long period of staleness that troubled him deeply. He felt as if all meaning had been drained from his life, and when he prayed, his prayers turned to chalk and died in his mouth before he could utter them. The rebbe, aware of his disciple's problem, took him out of the village to a deep, dark forest. Before they entered the forest, the rebbe said to the student, "As you are entering the forest, ask God to give you the answer to your dilemma, then forget about this prayer, because you must pay very close attention to the path through the forest. Otherwise you'll get lost and never come out of the forest alive." So the student entered the forest asking God for the answer to his struggle, and then he lost himself in following the path. As his rabbi had instructed him, he devoted all his attention to the path itself. Soon he began to take great pleasure in this path. He took pleasure in the working of his body as it found its own pace on the path and in the fall of his foot on the cool forest floor. He was taken with the path itself — a verdant mossy path of deep, brilliant green. When he finally came out of the forest, he was smiling broadly. The rebbe asked, "Did God give you an answer?" The student started to weep. "I forgot all about the question," he said. "I put all my attention on the path, and after a while I took so much pleasure in what was in front of my face that I forgot about the question altogether." "In that case," the rebbe said, "I would say that God gave you your answer."

The present moment is the only place we experience ourselves as being alive, the only place we experience our lives at all. The walk through the forest — the focus on the path, on the process of life, rather than on some goal or end that exists beyond the present-tense reality of our lives — this is the answer God provided for this student. You don't feel your life — your life is dead to you — because you aren't in it. If you want it to come alive again — if you want it to bristle with wonder and intensity — then you have to inhabit it, that dead, meaningless life that troubles you so. So inhabit your life. Be present in it, and watch the gray concrete turn a brilliant emerald green.

Sometimes we can't inhabit our lives because there's simply no room for us there. We might find our lives so clogged with dead weight — dead feelings, extraneous objects and concerns — that there's no room for the next live moment to occur.

The Torah has some excellent advice about how to nurture our spiritual passion in such a circumstance. It comes in the sixth chapter of Leviticus, in the instructions to the priests on how to keep the fire on the altar burning continually. "And he shall take up the ashes which the fire has consumed . . . and place them beside the altar, . . . and he shall remove the ashes outside the camp and the fire will be kept burning this way. It won't go out."

When we feel dead inside, it is often because there are old ideas we no longer believe in or haven't challenged in far too long, old feelings we really don't feel anymore but cling to desperately, afraid of what might happen if we admit we don't feel them. Without our realizing it, these things have suffocated us, crowding the life out of our soul. Sometimes they can be reinvigorated, refreshed, or reimagined. But sometimes they must be removed. We must simply let go of them. The altar must be emptied so that the light may keep burning. Shunryu Suzuki writes:

If your mind is empty, it is always ready for anything; it is open to everything. In the beginner's mind there are many possibilities; in the expert's mind there are few. . . . In the beginner's mind there is no thought, "I have attained something." All self-centered thoughts limit our vast mind. When we have no thought of achievement, no thought of self, we are true beginners.

This apparently was well understood by Rebbe Nachman, whose chronicler and close disciple Natan tells the following story:

—

When the rebbe was involved in his devotions, everything he did required great toil and effort. No form of devotion came easily, and the rebbe literally had to lay down his life in many cases. Each thing required tremendous effort. . . . He fell a thousand times, but each time he picked himself up and served God anew.

The most difficult thing was to begin serving God and accept the yoke of true devotion. Each time he would begin, he would find himself failing. He would then begin anew and stumble yet another time. This occurred countless times, over and over again.

Finally, the rebbe resolved to stand fast and maintain his foothold without paying attention to anything else in the world. From then on, his heart was firm in its devotion to God. But even so, he went up and down very many times.

But by then he was determined that he would never abandon his devotion, no matter how many times he fell. . . . The rebbe became accustomed to constantly beginning anew. Whenever he fell from his particular level, he did not give up. He would simply say, "I will begin anew. I will act as if I am just beginning to devote myself to God and this is the very first time."

This happened time and again, and each time, he would start all over again. He would often begin anew many times in a single day.

How frightening it is to consider that the ideas and feelings that used to motivate us — the very ones we based our lives on — are dead, no longer living ideas and feelings but dead ones that are cluttering up our lives, clouding our consciousness. After all, we have based our lives on these ideas and feelings, and if we have to give them up — if we have to let go of them — what do we do with our lives after that? Can we go on being a doctor if we don't have the same passion for healing we used to have? Can we continue to be a rabbi if all our theological assumptions have changed?

But the more urgent question might be, do we still have a life in the first place? Are we dead or alive? Are we still alive, or are we just breathing, merely going through the motions of our lives? And if so, what choice do we have but to give up these dead ideas; to inhabit our lives fully, even if they seem unappealing — even if that alternative life we might be living in Fairlawn, New Jersey, seems so much more alluring and attractive?

Choose life so that you may live. This is the great peroration of Parshat Netzavim. Live this life and watch it come alive again. This is also the great imperative of the Ten Days of Teshuvah, those days when we stand poised between life and death. While the gates are open, we can transform deadness into life; we can make the dead live again. We can choose life so that we may live.

Choose this life. There is no other.

—

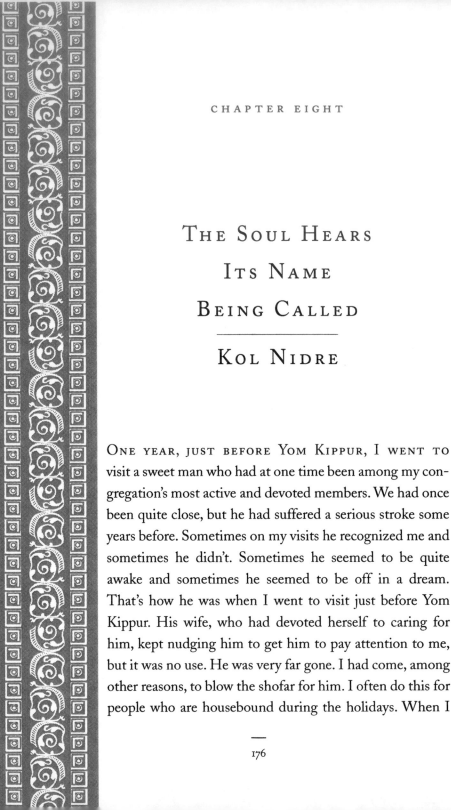

CHAPTER EIGHT

The Soul Hears
Its Name
Being Called

Kol Nidre

One year, just before Yom Kippur, I went to visit a sweet man who had at one time been among my congregation's most active and devoted members. We had once been quite close, but he had suffered a serious stroke some years before. Sometimes on my visits he recognized me and sometimes he didn't. Sometimes he seemed to be quite awake and sometimes he seemed to be off in a dream. That's how he was when I went to visit just before Yom Kippur. His wife, who had devoted herself to caring for him, kept nudging him to get him to pay attention to me, but it was no use. He was very far gone. I had come, among other reasons, to blow the shofar for him. I often do this for people who are housebound during the holidays. When I

—

176

blew the shofar for this man, he came to right away. It was as if the shofar had pulled him back to life, reached down into his dream and reclaimed his soul.

On another occasion, I was summoned to the house of a dying congregant. She had been the next-door neighbor and great friend of my predecessor, who was now dead himself. She wanted a rabbi present as she recited the Shemah with her last dying breath. I got to the house just in time. She began to recite the Shemah as soon as I arrived at her bedside. She was nearly gone, but she pulled herself back to this earth in order to say the first word. She said it with all her heart and all her soul and all her might, and then she sank back into her impending death for a moment. Then she said the second word, *Yisrael*, crawling all the way back up to the surface of this world in order to do so, only this time, it required super-human effort. And so it was through the six words of the Shemah. Each word seemed to pull her all the way up from death and back into life. She said the last word, *echad*, and then she died.

There are many ways to tell the story of how God called me back to Judaism, so whenever I tell this story, I tell it a little differently. The truth is, God had to call out to me many times, so sometimes I tell the story in terms of my involvement with Buddhism and how it made me more aware of who I really was and where I had come from. And sometimes I tell the story in terms of my marriage, how my wife and I decided to be married by a rabbi almost on a whim; how we began our observant Jewish life together on the first Shabbat after we were married. And sometimes I tell the story in terms of my son's sudden and surprising desire to have a Bar Mitzvah, and how that got me involved with a synagogue for the first time in my adult life almost against my will.

—

But long before any of that, way back in 1970, my first year in California, I was about as distant from Judaism as it was possible to be. How distant? It was the evening of Kol Nidre, the advent of Yom Kippur, and I had no idea that it was. But the TV was on in the living room of my house in Gualala, California, and I just happened to be walking through the room when a news broadcast caught my attention. They were doing a feature about Yom Kippur. Someone was playing the Kol Nidre on a cello. It went through me like a knife. That melody struck a deep chord. It went all the way in. It went straight to my soul.

Kol Nidre is the name of the service we perform on the eve of Yom Kippur. This service derives its name from the haunting chant with which it begins and which is also called the Kol Nidre. When we recite the Kol Nidre, God calls out to the soul, in a voice the soul recognizes instantly because it is the soul's own cry. You may have come to this service for other reasons. Nevertheless, here you are, sitting in your body, and suddenly your soul hears this music and it gives a jump, and it startles you. Your soul is hearing its name called out, and its name is pain, grief, shame, humiliation, loss, failure, death — or at least that is its first name. That is the name the first few notes of the Kol Nidre call out.

※

Kol Nidre has an interesting if somewhat cloudy history. It seems to have been composed during the reign of Reccared I, a sixth-century Visigoth king of Spain who ordered Jews to convert on pain of death. So Kol Nidre was originally a cry of pain, an expression of overwhelming grief at having had to commit apostasy. Spanish Jews chanted it when they gathered secretly to observe

Yom Kippur. They did the same later under the Byzantine per-secution of the ninth century, and again during the papal and Spanish Inquisitions of the thirteenth and fifteenth centuries. But I use the word *seems* advisedly. We're not really sure of any of this. The dates fit nicely, but there is no historical corroboration for this theory. It persists as a kind of folk myth. But it sure corre-sponds very closely to the feel of the Kol Nidre service: the soul is in anguish because it has encountered a frightening obstacle to expressing itself. But it resolves to persevere, and in so doing finds its true voice.

We can hear all this quite clearly in the music itself. The chant begins with a fall, a descending minor tone, which goes on for two full phrases, but then there is a definite rise. There is the sound of pain and heartbreak, but after that comes a kind of rising emotion, a heroic, even a defiant, persistence, and finally a kind of grim triumph.

Many years ago, at about the same time I heard that cello playing Kol Nidre, I had a friend who was learning the piano. She played Bach's First Prelude every day. This is a good piece for learning the piano because it essentially repeats one figure thirty-two times, altering the notes of the figure slightly with each repe-tition. The upper notes of this figure keep reaching higher and higher, ascending throughout the piece toward some great aspira-tion, but all the while this ascent is being subtly pulled down by a kind of gravity — the bass notes of this figure do not ascend, the high notes cannot pull them up, and finally even they begin to go down. As the high notes steadily ascend, a palpable tension builds between the ascent and the descent, until finally there is a heartbreaking moment in the music. The high notes give up; they

—

surrender to the bass notes, and they too begin to descend. One day, as I was listening to my friend rehearse this piece for the hundredth time, I heard the soul of all humankind in it. I heard the soaring aspirations of humanity, and I heard the force of a terrible gravity that finally brought it down. I heard the heart of all humankind cracking open.

The thing about the Kol Nidre is that it starts at this moment of heartbreak. This moment is its first assumption. And it comes on so suddenly, so abruptly. There is no buildup whatsoever. It's the very first thing that happens at the evening service for Yom Kippur. It happens before we even have a chance to settle in our seats. As the chant begins, we convene a Beit Din — a rabbinical court — and the first words of the chant are a legal formula. This court gives us permission to pray with the Avaryonim. What does this mean? Who are the Avaryonim and why does a court need to convene in order to give us permission to pray with them?

There is a strong and persistent folk belief that the word *Avaryonim* refers to the Marranos — the Jews of Spain who had pretended to convert to Christianity but had remained secretly Jewish and who returned to the Jewish community to say Kol Nidre every year. *Avaryonim*, the proponents of this theory argue, may very well have been a transliteration of the word *Iberians*.

Another theory is based on the talmudic dictum that a public fast in which sinners do not participate is not a true fast. *Avar*, after all, is the word for transgression. So perhaps the Avaryonim are the transgressors, and the rabbinical court is giving us permission to pray with them. In other words, it is giving us permission to pray with ourselves. We are all Avaryonim. We are all imperfect. We are all sinners.

But I think this word suggests an even deeper reality that all of us share. Not only are we all imperfect. We are all impermanent. In its simplest meaning, *Avar* means to pass. We are the Avaryonim. We are the ones who are just passing through, every one of us.

The tragic pain of the soul — the pain we hear in those first grieving notes of Kol Nidre — is the pain of loss, the pain of impermanence. This is the first hurdle the soul must clear as it makes its way through the world, the first disappointment it must come to grips with. Everything passes, everyone around us dies: the people we love, the things we love, the world around us, our parents, our grandparents, our children, our spouse, our strength, our capacities, the redwoods of California, the skyline of New York — all of it is sliding away, all this perfection sinking into the earth. And we know this. We try to hold on as hard as we can. We try to hold on to our strength and our youth, we try to hold on to each other. But we may as well try to hold back the waves of the sea. So this is the first note that is sounded in the song of the soul, and many of us never get past it.

One summer a group of us took a seven-day excursion into the deep wilderness of southeastern Alaska. We arrived in the wilderness during the end of the life cycle of the chum salmon. This is a remarkable cycle. The salmon rage up the wild rivers of Alaska to spawn, but the moment they do, they begin to lose their life force. They begin to die. They rage, they spawn, their life force dims, and they die. You can see this happening before your eyes.

Their scales begin to blacken and fall off. Their jaws become locked in a kind of permanent rage. And you can see it because something else happens in this final stage of their lives which is really quite wonderful. They begin to jump out of the water, very high and very often. This is extraordinary to see. Kayaking through Tebenkoff Bay in southern Alaska, we were constantly surrounded by salmon leaping out of the water.

Why do they do this? Some say it is a vestigial instinct left over from the days when they were running up the rivers and had to leap over many impediments. And some say they leap for joy, either the pure joy of the leap itself, or to celebrate that their lives have successfully run their course. They have spawned. They have kept the life cycle going. Someone on the trip said that they looked to him like pilgrims leaping from one dimension to the next — from earth to heaven — and then falling back again, stitching these dimensions together as they did.

This is nothing less than a picture of the journey the soul takes through this world. This is a picture of the soul's journey to express itself, to spawn, to create what it was put on this earth to create, and then to make a leap of great joy. And the soul makes this joyous leap in spite of the fact that it knows that as soon as it expresses itself, it will begin to die, it will begin to fade away. We rise up and we fall away. We express our unique and indispensable contribution to the great flow of life and then we pass on. We become one of the Avaryonim.

Yet many of us are afraid to be who we really are, precisely because we sense this. We sense that once we have risen up, we will begin to fall away. Once we have spawned, we will begin to die. Many of us would rather try to keep our lives unexpressed, in potential, because we believe that if we don't express our lives, we can hold on to them. Or we might be terrified of not expressing ourselves well enough, of failing. As long as we dream of that great novel we were always supposed to write, we never have to risk the unbearable tragedy of trying to write it and failing. Then where are we? Then what do we have? So we never make that joyous leap. We remain weighted down by the burden of our unexpressed dreams.

The Kol Nidre expresses all this. Those first notes express this sadness, this impermanence, this heartbreak, this failure. But then there are the rising notes. Precisely because of this impermanence, this heartbreak, the soul expresses itself, expresses its singular onetime gift, leaps out of the water with joy, and then expires.

Was it just me, or was all the hype and overkill we had to endure at the first anniversary of 9/11 just too much? I did my best to avoid it. I left the paper on the front stoop that day. I watched no TV except, of course, to tune in to the Giants game. But there was no escaping it. Even the Giants staged a memorial, and in spite of all my resistance, it ended up touching me deeply. It featured the simple, heartrending sound of bagpipes playing "Amazing Grace," while out in McCovey Cove people set a small flotilla of flowered wreaths afloat to honor the many victims of 9/11 who had lived in the Bay Area (Flight 93 was heading for San Francisco when its heroic passengers brought it down). And then there was the most beautiful touch of all. They didn't have anyone throw out a ceremonial first pitch as is often done on such occasions. Instead the mother of one of the victims merely laid the ball on the mound. The simple eloquence of this gesture called to mind the immensity of loss far more effectively than any words could have. And the keening of the bagpipes, like the Kol Nidre, was a cry of the soul, a cry of impermanence. The soul-numbing sadness of so much death could suddenly be felt. Never mind the theology, never mind the politics, never mind the cheap patriotism. That thin and lonely call of the pipes and that ball lying unthrown on the mound evoked the full sadness of this loss. But there was also a sense, as there is in the melody of the Kol Nidre, of the rise after the fall, of the soul engaging with its pain and then going on with its full strength, a strength strangely drawn from the pain itself. Eventually someone said, "Play ball," and they played ball. They picked up that ball and threw it, and the game went on.

About that salmon jumping again, and particularly the theory that the fish jumps as a vestigial instinct left over from the days when he was running the great rivers and leaping over impediments along the way. I think this image also tells us something about the soul's journey.

God calls to us from the depths of our despair. It is often the case, I think, that our soul hears its call in the midst of great trial and pain. The soul's journey through the world is a twisted and often painful path. But the soul seems to grow from its suffering, and from the impediments it encounters.

Rebbe Nachman said that when the soul hears its call and begins its journey back to God, God immediately begins to raise up impediments, because God knows that it strengthens the soul to overcome impediments, and because it is human nature — it is the nature of the soul — to yearn for precisely that which is difficult to attain.

My mother has been struggling with Alzheimer's disease for ten or twelve years now. I remember observing wistfully from the pulpit ten years ago that someday my mother was going to look at me and not even know who I was, not even recognize me. Well, that day has come, and it has been devastating, not only because of what it means in terms of my mother's condition, not only because it is as if I've already lost her even though she's still here, but because it touches a very deep nerve for me, a fear of not being recognized for who I am.

For many years I walked around in this world with a lot of anger toward my parents. My parents had always wanted me to be a doctor. There were only two alternatives for me in this world — to be a doctor or to be a failure. I tried to be accommodating. I took premed courses. I took chemistry, but I kept causing explosions and breaking expensive laboratory equipment, and finally the chemistry department offered me a deal: they would give me a passing grade in the chemistry class I was taking on the condition that I would promise never to take any more courses in the chemistry department. I accepted the deal, and that was the end of my medical career. It was just as well. My parents' desire to have me become a doctor had absolutely nothing to do with the person I actually was. They simply never saw that person. When I finally stopped trying to be who they wanted me to be and pursued my own path, my real talents began to emerge. I finished at the top of my graduate school class. I finished at the top of my class at rabbinical school, and my parents hardly noticed. I spent many years in a rage because of this, which was, I admit, a little silly. My parents were wonderful parents. They were loving and generous to a

—

fault, but this knot of pain and anger persisted. They just didn't see who I was, and it hurt me deeply. But one day I was sitting on a beach and it suddenly came to me: my soul had needed that struggle. It had needed to fight off my parents' idea of who I should be. It had needed to do this to become strong. It had needed to do this so that it could struggle up to the surface of the world and form itself in this struggle. It was, in fact, my parents' job to provide me with an impediment, to give my soul something to show its mettle against, something to prove itself against, something to express itself by overcoming.

The soul is pushed down and then the soul rises up again. The salmon leaps. This is precisely the struggle Kol Nidre depicts.

There is another cry of the soul later on in the liturgy of the Kol Nidre service. "Hear our voice, don't cast us out when we are growing old. When our strength begins to fail us, don't abandon us." And there is a similarly desperate cry in the Twenty-seventh Psalm, which we recite twice every day during the season of Teshuvah. "Even though my father and mother abandon me, you will be with me." And these, I now realize, are also songs that are sung to the soul. The soul is with us even when our father and mother don't see us or recognize us. And the soul is with us when our father and mother die and there is no one left to stand between us and death.

Now that my father is dead, when I go to the cemetery in New Jersey to visit him, we can finally meet soul to soul without any of the interference that used to characterize our relationship when he was still here. This is invariably a dazzling, radiant, affirming encounter, in the course of which my father is able to give me all the things he always wanted to give me but never could when he was alive, and I am able to receive all the things I always wanted from him but could never get.

Now my mother, having spawned us and lost her mate, has given up her life force. Twelve years into Alzheimer's, she can neither speak nor recognize her own children. She cannot walk or bathe or feed herself. She can only sit blankly by her living room window, humming along to tapes of old show tunes from the fifties, giggling at the chipmunks and bluebirds who pass by the window.

And my children now have risen up in the world. What kind of lives will they have? What kind of world will they live in? I worry about these things, and meanwhile I have already begun to fall away myself, although I still rage on, making long speeches, and writing, writing, furiously writing.

The song my soul recognizes, the song that gets my soul's attention, is a song of loss, at least those are the first notes of this song. They come upon me suddenly. Unexpectedly. I've barely had a chance to take my place. I've barely had a chance to settle into my own life, and yet there they are, those tragic notes pulling my soul from its scabbard.

And because my soul responds to this call, because my soul allows itself to hear it, because my soul recognizes its first name in these notes and does not shrink away nor withhold itself from them, when the next notes come, the ones that rise, I rise with them, in my full strength.

This song is a deep song, a song of great truth, a song of great strength, and I draw strength from it as I rise.

Thank God for this one run up the river, this blessed, silvery sliver of a moment in which we may express our divine gift or we may not.

Our soul is called to this world by a cry of pain, and then it rises, and that very pain met squarely and drunk in deeply can become its strength and, finally, its triumph.

※

Kol Nidre is about speaking true — about the power of speech. It is a gift to us from a time far back in our tribal consciousness when we seemed to understand these things better than we do now, when we seemed to understand the biblical warning that we are absolutely accountable for everything that comes out of our mouths.

In fact our ancestors took this so seriously that they instituted the Kol Nidre service to deal with it. They realized that it was a very serious thing to make a vow and not carry through with it, so here at the holiest moment of the year — here at the moment when the purity of our soul is a matter of life and death — they instituted a ritual for the annulment of vows, so that we wouldn't have to bear the guilt of abusing the power of speech.

The prominence of place given to speech in the Rambam's Law of Teshuvah is striking. These are the first words of this code:

When we commit a sin, whether intentional or unintentional, and then we make repentance, we are obliged to make confession [vidui] before God, and this confession must be in words. Even in the days of the Great Temple, when we brought sacrifices for our sins, either intentional or unintentional, the sacrifice did not atone for these sins unless we did Teshuvah, unless we made a verbal confession of them.

Later he writes:

And what is Teshuvah; we abandon our sin, and remove it from our thoughts, and resolve in our hearts that we won't do it anymore. We repent of the past, and proclaim before the knower of all purposes that we won't return to this kind of behavior again. And we need to make this confession with our lips moving; to say these things out loud that we have resolved in our heart.

But the Rambam makes clear that these must not be empty words. If we make verbal confession without sincerely resolving to change in our hearts, he insists, we are like someone who goes into the mikvah (the purifying bath) with a sheretz (an impure insect) in his hand. We can't be purified while we are holding on to impurity, and we can't make Teshuvah while our heart holds on to our misdeeds either. And not only does this confession have to be heartfelt, but according to the Rambam, it must be specific, and it is praiseworthy to make confession in public as well.

So clearly, verbal confession is basic to the process of Teshuvah.

In the last chapter, we looked at the verse from Parshat Netzavim that describes the process of Teshuvah so precisely. The commandment to do Teshuvah "is not distant from you," the Torah insists. "The word is very near to you, in your mouth and in your heart, so you can do it." And in the chapter on Elul I noted how the contents of the heart defy direct examination but will often reveal themselves unbidden when we are trying to focus on something else. So, I suggested, a good way to catch a glimpse of precisely what is in our hearts is to watch, to become mindful of what keeps carrying our attention away as we try to focus on the words of the High Holiday prayer book. Or we might focus on our breath or our body instead, and watch what comes up then.

Every spiritual tradition I am aware of speaks of a kind of layered mindfulness, a sensibility that works up and out of the body, to the heart and then to the mind and then finally to the soul. The Buddhist sutra On Mindfulness describes this kind of layered grid of awareness, and the Kabala, the Jewish mystical tradition, speaks of it too. According to the Kabala, we start out with our awareness in Asiyah — the world of physicality, the world of the body, our most immediately accessible reality. Then we become aware of the heart, Yetzirah — the world of formation or emotion, that shadowy world between conception and its realization in material form. From there we move on to the world of pure intellect, Briyah, or creation, and then to Atzilut, the realm of pure spiritual emanation.

But it's that first step which concerns us the most at this time of year; moving from the body to the heart, focusing on the reality of our present circumstances and letting the contents of our heart come welling up in the process.

So the first order of business in this process of Teshuvah is becoming aware of the heart, either by direction or indirection. But this is only half the equation. We must also *speak* of what we find there. By bringing our awareness out of our hearts and into speech, by moving this consciousness outward to the light of the great world outside, we complete the process.

Every year, just before Yom Kippur, I make a concerted effort to speak out the shadowy contents of my heart to another human being. I usually find myself speaking of things I have thought of a thousand times before — of my anger, of my obstinacy, of my refusal to give up the grudges I hold against people. I know these things as well as I know the back of my own hand. I have thought these thoughts a thousand times before. Still, to get them *out* makes a tremendous difference. I know them, but as long as they are unspoken, I can ignore them. I don't have to act on them. Now that I have said them out loud to another human being, they are out there in the world. It would be much harder to ignore them anymore; harder to deny them; harder to act in a way that failed to take them into account.

This, I believe, is the basis of psychotherapy. We speak our unconscious dysfunctions, and in so doing we disarm them. We call them out. We bring them up to the light of day, where, like the ancient river demons of the Near East, they lose their power. On a certain level, of course, we always know what we are doing. But as long as it remains unspoken, we can pretend to ignore it. The veil of unconsciousness is very thin, however, and as soon as we begin to speak, we pierce it, and we can't ignore what we were doing any longer.

Speech is one of our distinctive human attributes. It is through speech that we make the inner, outer; that we bring the metaphysical into the physical; that we make real the purely intellectual. It is through speech that action begins. Every time I speak, it is the result of something metaphysical arising in my soul as an idea or a spiritual impulse. It becomes speech in my mouth and then goes out onto the air of the room as a wave — a part of the

—

world of Asiyah, the physical world. Then it enters someone else's ear and then their mind, where it is transformed into something metaphysical again. All this is a truly miraculous transaction and a decisively human power. And think of how intimately it joins us to those to whom we are speaking. Think of the intimate access it gives us to their inner lives and vice versa.

And speech is intimately joined to the power of gesture as well. Jean Piaget, the great child psychologist, based all his theories about child development on acute firsthand observation. He never obtained any advanced degrees. Rather, he got down on the floor and watched children with a focused, unwavering eye. Down on the floor, he watched closely as a young girl developed the ability to speak. He noticed that before she began to speak, she communicated by gesture. When she wanted to communicate the idea of "no," she shook her head and waved a closed fist across her chest. When she first began to speak, the gesture was still quite pronounced — she said "no" and she shook her head and she waved her fist across her body. As her speaking became more refined, the gesture began to get smaller and smaller, and finally it almost disappeared altogether: almost, but never completely. There was always at least a vestige of this gesture in her speech — an almost imperceptible waver of the head, a twitching of the hand. Piaget saw this pattern replicated in hundreds of children. For all of them, there was some sort of gesture before speech, and a gesture that remained afterward also. That's why we feel speech so intensely. It always retains the force of this primal gesture.

And that is how speech is connected to the primary, prelingual world — a world of great power. How did God create the world? Through speech. God said, Let there be light, and there was light. God said, Let there be dry land on the waters, and there was dry land. The one exception was us. We were created by breath. God created us by breathing air into our nostrils, and according to Rebbe Nachman, this means that we are directly connected to God through our breath. Our breath connects us to the level of experience that is deeper than speech, deeper than the forms speech creates — not the word for the thing, but the thing itself. Breath has primacy over speech. We can breathe without speaking, but we can't speak without breathing.

The kind of speech the Rambam refers to is speech that arises from the breath, speech that expresses this primary sense of reality. When our speech expresses this deeper sense of things, we are on our way to Teshuvah. We are on our way to bringing that which is in our hearts out into the world. Speech that is not so connected is to no avail, at least not where Teshuvah is concerned. It is like a person in the ritual bath holding on to an impure insect.

Ten years ago the state of California reinstituted the death penalty. Ten executions have been carried out at San Quentin prison, just outside of San Francisco, since then, and I have attended each of these in protest. Many others have come to protest these executions also, and we have gotten to know each other. One of them is a remarkable woman named Aba Gail.

Eighteen years ago, Catherine Blount, Aba Gail's youngest daughter, was living with a friend, a young man named Eric, sharing an old farmhouse outside Auburn, California, in the hills above Sacramento. Eric had a best friend named Douglas. They were both Vietnam vets, and both had gotten heavily involved in drugs while in Vietnam. Back in the States, Eric managed to clean himself up. Douglas never could. Now he was pretty seriously

—

strung out and prone to psychotic, paranoid delusions. Finally he came to believe that his friend Eric had stolen his power as a human being, and that the only way he could survive was to kill Eric. So Douglas went up to Auburn and murdered his friend Eric, and he killed Catherine Blount too, simply because she happened to be in the house when he got there.

It was a horrible crime, a grisly, senseless double murder, and there was absolutely no question as to Douglas's guilt. For eight years afterward, Aba Gail was consumed with anger and rage. She screamed in the shower every day. She cried every time she was alone. She couldn't even drive a car, because as soon as she was alone behind the wheel she would start to cry so hard she couldn't see the road.

The sheriff's department told her that they were going to find the culprit, convict him, and execute him. Then, they assured her, she would have peace. She believed them. She felt she had to hurt someone for what had been done to her daughter, and she thought that once she did, she would feel better.

This went on for eight years. Douglas was arrested, and then he was convicted, but there was no peace for Aba Gail in this, and she began to realize for a certainty that there would be no peace when he was executed either.

Finally something turned in her, and she realized she would never find any peace until she could forgive Douglas. It took her four more years to be able to do it. She took small steps at first. She signed up for a meditation class. She started reading books. Then it became a full-time obsession. For four years, she never read a novel or a magazine. She never watched TV or went to the movies. She studied voraciously. She studied Buddhism, Hinduism, and the

Jewish teachings on forgiveness. She soaked everything up like a sponge. But still her heart was full of pain, rage, and violence.

She thought that she had actually forgiven Douglas at one point, but she still felt no peace. One of her friends told her her forgiveness would never be real unless she verbalized it to Douglas, but that only made Aba Gail furious. She even stopped speaking to this friend for a while. What do you mean, tell him? I don't have to tell him. I know what's going on in my own heart.

But shortly after that, four years after she felt that mysterious turning in her breast, and twelve years after her daughter's murder, Aba Gail heard a voice, an inner voice, but a voice as loud and as clear as any she had ever heard in her life. It said, You must forgive him and you must *tell him* you forgive him. You must speak it to him.

Aba Gail complied. She sat down immediately and wrote Douglas the following note: "Dear Douglas, The spirit of God in me sends a blessing to the spirit of God in you." Then she put the letter in the mailbox, and as soon as she did, she felt healed. She felt herself to be in a state of grace, and she has felt that way ever since.

Now all this happened unconsciously and unintentionally, on the level of instinct. True, four years before, she had embarked on the path of forgiveness. But she had never said to herself, I am full of pain. This anger is destroying me. She had simply heard the voice, written her words, sent them out, then immediately felt how much these things had been true, how full of pain she had been for those twelve years since her daughter had been murdered — how much her anger had been destroying her inside. She felt this all quite clearly in the way she felt the moment before and the way

—

she felt the moment after she wrote to Douglas. She felt the physiological damage that violence and anger and rage had done to her. She felt what it had done to her body, her mind, her soul, her family. And she felt the heroic effort her soul had made to let all of this go, and she knew for a certainty that she had been healed, that she had been able to bring all this up and then let it out the moment she had gotten the words out, the moment she had put the words to paper and then sent them away, the moment she had spoken true.

The Kol Nidre is also a voice, an ancient voice, but one that still calls to us. We can hear its message in this poem by Paul Celan:

> Speak, you too,
> speak as the last,
> say out your say.
> Speak —
> But don't split off No from Yes.
> Give your say this meaning too:
> give it the shadow.
> Give it shadow enough,
> give it as much
> as you know is spread round you from
> midnight to midday and midnight.
> Look around:
> see how things all come alive —
> By death! Alive!
> Speaks true who speaks shadow.

The path of transformation is long and it is arduous. We spend weeks and months, peering into our hearts, feeling the heft of our shadow and the hurt in our soul.

Then Kol Nidre comes, and it is finally time to speak of those thoughts and feelings that haunt us. Somewhere in the twenty-four hours of Yom Kippur, we must speak the shadow. We must speak it in private and we must speak it in public. We must speak it to a friend or speak it to a stranger. We must speak it to a husband or a wife. We must speak it in the shadow language of our own heart, or speak it through the liturgy, the communal unburdening of the Vidui, the confessional prayer we recite over and over again during these twenty-four hours.

The Kol Nidre is calling us. It is saying, Speak. Speak the shadow, as much as you know is spread around you midnight to midday to midnight. Speak and let go. Speak and be human. Speak and be healed.

א

Every year, around ten weeks before Kol Nidre, we read a strange foreshadowing of this night in the Torah, in Parshat Matot. Parshat Matot begins with a discussion of vows, in which we hear the precise language of Kol Nidre. "When a man makes a vow to God or swears an oath which is binding on his soul, all vows and all bonds on his soul shall stand [*cal nidareyah vcal isar asher asrah al nafshah yakum*]." I always get a chill of fear in my spine when we read this. It's the first distant echo of the High Holidays, of Kol Nidre. What will I do this year? What will I say to the congregation?

The irony is that the subject of both Parshat Matot and Kol Nidre is the relationship between what we say and what we do. Both the Torah and the rabbis of the Talmud believed in the primacy of language, in the mysterious power of language to create a reality.

In the account of creation we read every year in the Book of Genesis, God literally speaks the world into existence. And the Talmud affirms the creative potential of speech. Did you know that *abracadabra* is a Jewish word? The Aramaic words *Avra c'dabrah* mean "It came to pass as it was spoken," a popular talmudic dictum that expressed the widely held talmudic belief that things do indeed come to pass because they are spoken, that speech has the power to cause the world to come into being.

On Kol Nidre we affirm that it is an absolute catastrophe, it throws the soul out of balance, to have our words out of line with our deeds. But it is also an inevitable catastrophe, so every year at the beginning of this great ritual day in which we purify our souls, we remedy this: we forgive ourselves in advance for all the times in the coming year when we will make vows we will be unable to keep, when our words will be out of line with our deeds, and we acknowledge in this ritual that these times will certainly and inevitably come.

Parshat Matot deals with one very particular instance of this: the case in which a woman makes a vow she can't keep because she is living under the power of a man — either her husband or her father — who won't let her keep it. The Torah's remedy in such a case is to forgive the woman for not keeping her vow.

This is an interesting passage for a number of reasons. For one thing, it is a very good example of how the authors of the

Torah (divine and/or human) mediated its values with the realities of human life. The Torah has a very strong sense of what is, and an equally strong sense of what ought to be, and it recognizes very clearly that if the second ever gets too far away from the first, the Torah will become a repository of irrelevant and impossible ideals. So it is that the Torah will often leave an institution standing, even one it abhors, and simply try to infuse that institution with its values, rather than do away with it altogether. If it does the latter, it will place itself at too great a distance from the society it is trying to transform.

The Torah clearly has the idea that every human being needs to have absolute freedom of choice. Otherwise the religious system the Torah introduces couldn't possibly work. It recognized that in a social system where women lived under the power of men, they didn't have this kind of freedom, but it sensed the futility of trying to overthrow this system overnight. So it simply expressed its values and left the system intact, trusting that in another two or three thousand years the value would work its magic on the system and the system would give way — avra c'dabrah. This, of course, is precisely what has happened. The attitude the Torah expresses toward women may not be consistent with contemporary values of gender equality, but the fact of the matter is, it is the beginning of these contemporary values, of the vectorial movement that resulted in them. The women of the Torah were oppressed, but by subtly indicating its unhappiness with their oppression, the Torah began to undo it.

But all this operates on another level as well. This I learned from the commentaries of Ibn Gikitilla, the great medieval Spanish Kabalist. Gikitilla saw this whole business as a *remez*, a mystical hint at the secret workings of the psyche. The woman in question here, according to Gikitilla, was not an actual person, but rather the *neshamah* — the soul, the feminine representation of the will of God, the *tzelem elohim*, the image of God that resides deep in every human soul. The man whose power it lives under is the *yetzer hara* — the evil impulse — which often prevents the neshamah from making its will manifest.

This is really quite a useful metaphor from several points of view.

First, it tells us that action really does spring from a kind of inner speech, the language we use to define the world to ourselves. Like God, each of us participates in the creation of the world. Blessed be He who speaks and the world comes into being, we say of God in our liturgy every morning. But it applies to us as well. We also speak and bring the world into being. The world presents us with a great chaos of information. Our speech encourages us to select certain possibilities out of this chaos and to discard others. Not only that, but this deep inner speech that precedes action is always well intentioned, always comes from the neshamah, that deep inner echo of the word of God.

But this deep inner voice often fails to make it to the surface of the world in the form of action because of the tumultuous whirlwind of impulses it encounters between the heart and the world. This, in fact, is what Gikitilla identifies as the yetzer hara, that complex of impulses and dysfunctions that so often prevents us from doing what we know we should do.

As accurate as this picture of the soul — of our inner life — might be, what is really impressive about Gikitilla's teaching is the prescription he suggests. What do we do when this man — this yetzer hara — prevents this woman living under his power — the *neshamah* — from manifesting her vow, from manifesting the divine speech at the base of all human action? We do the same thing that the Torah suggests we do in the human case: we recognize that there was nothing the woman could do about it, or in other words, that there is really nothing *we* can do about it when our complex of impulses and dysfunctions prevents us from doing what we know we should do. There is no blame in this, Gikitilla insists. It is like a vow that cannot be fulfilled because we are living under someone else's power.

But actually, Gikitilla suggests, there is something we can do about it. We can strengthen the woman, the neshamah, so that she can express her full strength. How do we do this? By doing spiritual work, by practicing spiritual discipline, by meditating, by performing religious rituals, performing Tzedakah and Gemilut Chasadim — charity and acts of loving-kindness. When we do these things, we strengthen the neshamah, we let her have her way, and sooner or later she finds herself able to overcome the yetzer hara and make her will manifest in the world.

So it is that the historical reality the text recognizes is mirrored very precisely in the realm of the soul. It is mirrored in our lives as well.

My dear friend and partner at the Makor Or meditation center, Norman Fischer, was counseling a man a few years ago. This man had been walking around with a grudge, with hatred in his heart that he just couldn't get rid of. He had recently moved to a new town in the East Bay, and one day a neighbor told a racist joke in his presence and he didn't laugh. Instead, he gently told this man that he didn't like racist jokes and asked him please not to say anything like that in his presence in the future.

But just to show that there was nothing personal in this, some time later, he invited this man and his wife to have dinner with him and his wife at their home. The neighbor and his wife came and they all sat down to a lovely dinner, whereupon this fellow proceeded to unleash a bitter torrent of abuse on his unsuspecting host. "I don't like you, and no one else around here likes you either. You just don't get it and you never will," he said.

They all managed to limp through the rest of the evening somehow, but ever since then, this student of Norman's had been walking around with a great bitterness toward his neighbor, a simmering anger, constantly eating away at him. So now he was coming to Norman for advice on how he might get rid of these feelings.

I don't know if Norman viewed his student's story as skeptically as I did. I don't know if he wondered, as I did, if there wasn't some hostility in his having the neighbor to his house for dinner in the first place; if he hadn't done it so that he could feel superior to him. Maybe the neighbor sensed this and that's why he was so hostile at the dinner table. Maybe Norman's student felt bitter toward this man before he was insulted over his own dinner table. Maybe that's why he was having such a hard time overcoming this bitterness.

What I do know is that Norman promptly advised his student to stop trying to get rid of these feelings. After all, they were his feelings. They were his reality, and there are no alternative realities. This is what was welling up from the inner recesses of his soul, from the neshamah. Why not let her have her way? Instead of trying to get rid of these feelings, Norman suggested, why not forgive himself for having them?

And having so forgiven himself, why not try to inhabit these feelings as deeply as he could, why not unleash them and give them free rein? Maybe then, Norman said, he might find himself following these feelings all the way to the core of his being, and to the deep well of suffering there. This, after all, was not just his suffering — not just his anger and pain — but the bottomless and endless suffering that lay at the core of all human experience, the same suffering that had led the neighbor to tell the racist joke and then to insult him at his own dinner table in front of his wife. Finally, this sense of suffering might give way to a deep and abiding compassion, the compassion that usually comes when we realize that we and our fellow human beings are all fellow sufferers.

If Ibn Gikitilla had heard Norman give this advice, first of all, I'm quite sure he would have agreed, and second, I think he would have understood it this way. He would have understood Norman to be advising his student to forgive himself for his anger and the grudge he bore the other man. The student may very well have vowed to himself not to live by anger, not to bear grudges, but he was under the power of impulses that made it impossible for him to fulfill this vow. So what he needed to do was to strengthen his neshamah, and the way to do this was to let her have her way, to inhabit her as completely as he could. If he did this, perhaps it would lead him to the word of God at her root, to the suffering that unites us all, and to the abiding compassion that always seems to come on the heels of the recognition of this suffering.

—

Spiritual discipline can help us make this transformation. Meditation is a time when we inhabit ourselves this way. Shabbat is too. So is daily prayer, or any kind of daily spiritual discipline. Work, TV, and our usual frantic rush of activities are all devices we use to distract ourselves from ourselves, to keep from looking at who we are, to keep from fully inhabiting ourselves. Most of us are afraid to inhabit ourselves, afraid of what we might find at the core of our being. This is how we are caught unprepared.

According to Gikitilla, this fear is the yetzer hara, the man under whose power we live, the one who prevents us from fulfilling the deepest vows of the soul. Shabbat and meditation give the neshamah free rein. They strengthen the neshamah so that she can overcome this fear. They strengthen the neshamah until we can finally hear her voice.

We hear this voice in the Kol Nidre. We hear the inner logarithm by which we define ourselves. Hearing this, we can forgive ourselves. Hearing this, there is nothing to be afraid of anymore. Hearing this, we are prepared to speak this world into being. *Avra c'dabrah.*

✣

Who are the Avaryonim? Addressing this question earlier, we mentioned the possibility that the Avaryonim are the sinners, the imperfect among us. The word *avar,* after all, means to sin or to transgress. Someone might say, "We can't pray with the imperfect. This is a very important time, and only those who are morally unblemished should pray now. All those others — all those imperfect ones — will prevent our prayers from being answered."

But the Beit Din — the rabbinical court — comes to say, There is no such thing as a morally unblemished human being. There are only Avaryonim — only the imperfect and the incomplete — so not only are we permitted to pray with them, we are required to. Pray we must, and there is simply no one else to pray with And besides, it is precisely because we are Avaryonim that we need each other so. Since each of us is imperfect by nature — since each of us is incomplete — it is only in community that we begin to find a sense of wholeness, a sense of completion. So not only is it permissible, not only is it required, for us to pray with the Avaryonim — the imperfect ones — we have a desperate need to do so. In praying with them we begin to find the answer to our own imperfection.

None of us is whole by ourselves. A spiritual community is one in which we find wholeness, completion with others. What we lack is provided by somebody else. Now I know, this is a positively un-American idea. The John Wayne in us balks at it furiously. We are indoctrinated by our culture to see ourselves as self-sufficient. One of the hardest things I have to do as a rabbi is to convince people who are ill or in trouble to accept help from others. In this culture, needing help from others is seen as a sign of weakness, as something to be ashamed of.

But I think that deep down we all know — we all understand intuitively — that none of us is whole by ourselves. And this understanding is the basis of spiritual community. We all seem to know in the deepest part of ourselves that we need to be part of something larger than ourselves to be complete.

A couple of months ago, I was driving on the central freeway in heavy traffic, when all of a sudden a small red car jammed full of teenagers came speeding up an entrance ramp, crossed three lanes of traffic without even slowing down, and forced an old Volkswagen bug off the road and onto the median strip at the center of the freeway. I watched this happen in horror, but it only got worse. With the Volkswagen still up on the median strip, the red car sped away as fast as it could, the kids in the backseat laughing hysterically as it did. I was incensed. I took off after the red car at high speed until I got close enough to write down its license plate number. Then I slowed down and waited for the Volkswagen to catch up to me. It came by a few minutes later. The woman driving it was weaving all over, as if in a daze. I followed her till she got off the freeway at Fell Street, flagged her down, told her I had seen the whole thing, gave her the license number and my card, and told her to call me if she needed a witness. A few weeks later the following letter arrived in the mail:

Three years ago, I was assaulted and sustained severe injuries. I'm still suffering the consequences of that attack. So when I was assaulted by that vehicle on August 5, it felt like the same thing was happening all over again. The difference was that last time, nobody saw, and this time, you saw the whole thing and took the time and energy to follow me off the freeway. Your involvement was psychologically healing for me. Thank you for making a connection with me and giving credence and integrity to the event. I am very grateful.

I don't tell you this story to brag about what a great guy I am (at least, not only for that reason). The truth is, my following that car that day probably had more to do with a generalized rage against teenagers on my part than with my virtue. But I think this story makes a profound and important point. We are all Avary-onim, incomplete in ourselves. It takes the presence of other people to make us whole — to give credence and integrity to our experience. According to Rabbi Abraham Joshua Heschel, even God had that need — even God needed a witness to lend integrity and credence to the creation — and that, apparently, is why God created us. So if God has this need, how can we be ashamed of it — how can we see ourselves as being above it?

❧

Let me tell you about the best day I've had in a long time. As I describe it, you are going to think I am crazy, and no doubt I am. This may not seem like a very good day to you at all, especially at first.

The day began with a prayer minyan, as many of my days do. The service was particularly beautiful and strong that morning, and I felt my ego dissolving into the prayers even more than I usually do.

I spent the rest of the morning doing pastoral visits. First I went out to Marin County to see a woman who had been sick for a long time and was now terribly depressed. She was angry at her illness, taking it out on her family, terribly down, refusing to move out of bed, and insisting that people leave her alone and let her sleep all the time. She was furious at her husband for trying to get her out of bed, and now especially furious with him because he had arranged my visit. Nevertheless, it was remarkable how she roused herself for my visit, how the appearance of someone from the outside lifted her energy and made her come out of herself in a way she hadn't been able to do by herself.

I left her and went to the hospital to see one of our regulars who had had a difficult surgery just the week before and was not recovering well. She was seriously depleted, barely communicating and terribly despondent. But I was able to tell her that everyone from the synagogue was thinking of her and that we were continuing to pray for her, and I could feel her spirit lifting when I said this. It was very real, a palpable feeling.

There was another woman, from Long Island, at the same hospital. She had come to our synagogue the week before her surgery was scheduled and had asked me if I would visit her afterward. Her surgery had not gone so well, and she was also terribly discouraged, and now she needed blood — lots of it. I told the woman who runs the synagogue blood drive, and she managed to get ten people from our synagogue — all with the right blood type — down to the hospital within hours. The woman and her family were overwhelmed. They had felt such a deep sense of need, and our community — their community, in the larger sense — had answered it.

Finally, I saw another person in despair. A woman who had suddenly fallen ill, and who had lost faith in her capacity to get well again, even though medically there was every reason to expect she would recover. I sat by her bed and told her over and over again how much I loved her — how much everyone in the community loved her — and that we would never abandon her no matter what. Although her despair did not lift, I could see that she was beginning to draw strength from this reminder that our community was still there, and still mindful of her. And I noticed something else, this time about myself. Although it was very difficult to see this woman so reduced by her illness, it felt wonderful nevertheless to be telling her that I loved her, that we all loved her, that we would never let her go. It gave me a great deal to be able to say these things to her.

Still, at the middle of the day as I went home to quickly change my clothes, what did I have? I had four people, one more ill than the next, and none of them quite able to summon the will to go on, none of them with the faith that their life was worth living, none of them quite believing in their lives or in life in general.

Then I got in the car and drove up to Healdsburg as quickly as I could to do a wedding. The traffic was bad and I was already a little late. I do a lot of weddings these days, and I love to do them. It is such a deep and intimate thing to share with people. Set against the deep discouragement about life, the deep despair I sense in our society, especially among young people, there is nothing so optimistic as a wedding, nothing which says, "In spite of appearances, I believe life is good and the world will go on," so forcefully as this.

Since I was so late, the wedding began almost as soon as I arrived. We signed the wedding contract — the Ketuvah — very quickly, and then we went out to stand under the wedding canopy — the chuppah. The chuppah had been erected in the middle of one of the loveliest vineyards in Sonoma County. It was an incredibly beautiful day — bright sun, blue skies. But the wind was blowing very hard. The Ketuvah was now resting on an easel next to the chuppah, and the wind blew it over several times, and it kept blowing my kippah, my skullcap, off my head, and it was positively tearing through the cloth top of the chuppah. I thought it was going to blow us away altogether, but it never did. We just kept picking up the Ketuvah, I kept putting my kippah back on my head, and the chuppah miraculously held. The Hebrew word for wind is *ruach*. It also means spirit or soul. And the truth was, there was even more ruach, more spirit, inside that chuppah than out. My feelings are always very intense under the chuppah, but this was something else again — something more powerful than I had ever felt before.

And suddenly I understood what I was feeling. I was feeling that this beautiful young couple standing before me was manifesting the affirmation for life that the four sick people I had been with earlier in the day could not manifest. I felt that in some strange way they were manifesting it for them; that the resounding "yes" this couple was now saying to life had somehow come out of the four sick ladies I had seen earlier in the day. It was their missing piece. It was their voice in the wind, something so deep it could only be said by all the people I had seen that day — by a whole community — and not by any particular person.

That young couple in Healdsburg had no way of knowing, of course, but I was quite convinced that the reason the feeling under their chuppah was so strong, so deep, was because it included the despair of these four ladies and in fact transformed that despair. And the four ladies had no idea, but this young couple saying yes to the world with the wind blowing furiously all around them, was saying yes for them, saying what they needed to say but could not quite manage to say. So they were all Avaryonim — the four sick women and the young couple getting married — and they were praying together, and taken together their prayer spread a canopy of deep peace over the Sonoma hills.

The Kol Nidre is also such a prayer. It is a prayer that calls the soul back to itself, a prayer that calls the soul to its real home, and that home is always in something larger than itself. We are Avaryonim. We are incomplete and imperfect and cannot survive without a spiritual community that can make us whole — that can give us what we need, what we don't have.

And what we need most of all is to give. We need to give what we have and someone else does not. We are not John Wayne; we are the Avaryonim. And that sense of wholeness, of completion, that we have been chasing after all of our lives — but that always eludes us as individuals — is something so deep it can only be found in a whole community, in that shifting composite of need and lack and gift we create when we come together to acknowledge that we need each other.

The Kol Nidre calls the soul to its community and to its rightful place in this great, shifting sea of life.

CHAPTER NINE

DEATH AND
YOM KIPPUR ATONE

ONE SUNDAY MORNING SOME YEARS AGO, I WAS
rushing out the door to the airport on my way to a rabbinical conference, when I received an emergency call from the
Board of Rabbis hotline.

A woman, quite distraught, was on the line. She had
given birth to a baby boy that morning, but he had been
born without most of his brain, and she'd been told he
would die that afternoon. She wasn't married to the boy's
father — he was a Catholic, and a priest had already been
called in to perform a baptism. Now the mother and her
parents, who were Jewish, wanted something Jewish done.

They were at the University of California–San
Francisco Medical Center, so I stopped in on my way to the

—

airport. The baby was in the intensive care nursery, a room I'd never been in before. It was like a hothouse. The temperature was kept at over ninety degrees.

What did they want done? As the woman and her parents spoke, it seemed clear that it was important to them that the baby have a name. According to Jewish law, we don't name a baby until it has been alive for at least a week, but this seemed like a bad time to stand on Halakah. They had already formed a strong bond with this child, and it was important to them that he have an identity, a Jewish identity. They also seemed to want some sort of last rites performed. And so it was that I ended up doing one of the strangest and saddest things I have ever had to do as a rabbi: saying the blessings for the beginning of life and the end of life in one breath — in a single prayer. First I said the prayer for naming a child that is usually part of a Brit Milah (ritual circumcision), and then I said the final prayer a Jew says in life — the Vidui, the last confession. I said them as one long prayer.

We named the child Baruch, a blessing. Everyone in the room — the woman, the baby's Catholic father, both sets of grandparents — everyone had the strange sense about this tragic and radiant child that he was perfect, that this was a brief but perfect life — not perfect in the sense of being the best, not in a comparative sense, but in the sense of being absolutely what it was. This was a perfect life, a life without a brain or any duration to speak of, a life begun and ended in a single breath.

The rabbis had an expression — *k'fitzat ha derech*, a shortening of the way. It expressed a sense of telescoping a journey, the sense of crossing an impossible distance in a few brief strides. And being in the presence of a life that rushed so precipitously called to mind the terror of my own end. This life was a synopsis of all life; we are born and we die, and nothing that happens in between is nearly as important as these two fundamental facts of life. And there was something else I felt that day, which I have often felt, before and after, but never quite so strongly as that morning in the intensive care nursery at UCSF, and that is that once life is over, it is clear that it has taken up no time or space at all. I often stand with people at the last moment of their life, and I always feel this. Whether they are eight days old or eighty-nine years, the moment life is gone it is nowhere, neither in time nor in space. In the words of the psalmist, "The days of a human being are like the grass. We flourish as a flower in the field, then a wind passes over and we are gone. No one can even see the place where we were anymore."

All the world is a narrow bridge, Rebbe Nachman said, a narrow bridge between the nothingness at the beginning and the nothingness at the end. We spend our whole lives on this precarious span, unaware that we are even on it. Then one day we wake up and see it, and we feel terror. We say to ourselves, My God, what have I been doing with my life?

The High Holidays are also a bridge, a compressed journey — *k'fitzat ha derech* — the voyage from birth to death in ten days' time. Rosh Hashanah is all about birth, and Yom Kippur is about death. Rosh Hashanah is Yom Harat Ha-Olam, the Day the World Is Born, and Yom Kippur is the day we rehearse for our death by wearing a shroud and by abstaining from life-affirming activities, like eating and sexuality.

But perhaps the most profound connection between death and Yom Kippur is the mysterious claim the Talmud makes for both of them: both Yom Kippur and death atone. We say the Vidui, the final confession, on two occasions in our lives — on Yom Kippur and on the day of our death. The word for atonement — Kippur, *kaparah* — means a covering over. Death is a covering over. Sometimes I feel this quite literally at the graveyard. I know that many people have a fear of being buried. But sometimes when we are shoveling the dirt over a casket at the cemetery, I get the feeling that we are covering our loved one over with earth as we would cover a baby with a blanket. The vast blankness of death covers over all our wrongdoing in this life, and the communal chanting of the Vidui on Yom Kippur — this sea of shared acknowledgment, this commonality of wrongdoing — seems to cover over our individual sin as well.

But most of us are singularly uncomforted by the prospect of being forgiven upon our death. While we are acting out this pageant of the journey from birth to death, there is Moses, in the Torah, in the background of our communal consciousness, dying quietly but clinging to life with everything he has. We often read Parshat Vayelech the week before Yom Kippur. This Torah portion begins with Moses once again pleading to be allowed to live and to enter the Promised Land. Between the lines of this text, the Midrash perceives a titanic struggle between Moses and God. God seals the decree against Moses and swears by the Ineffable Name that Moses will not enter the Promised Land.

Moses then utters more than fifteen hundred prayers. He draws a circle around himself and stands at the center and proclaims, "I will not move from this spot until the judgment against me is suspended." God promptly orders every gate in heaven locked, lest Moses' prayers find an opening.

The prayers are fruitless in the end, and when Moses sees this, he begs heaven and earth, the sun and the moon, the stars and the planets, the mountains and the rivers, and finally the sea itself to intercede for him, to no avail.

Finally God asks: "Why are you so aggrieved at your impending death?" And Moses answers: "I am afraid of the sword of the Angel of Death — of the pain of death itself." God replies: "If that's the reason, then don't worry; I won't deliver you to the Angel of Death." But Moses still clings desperately to life. A few hours before his death, God says to him: "How long will you endeavor in vain to avert your death? You have only three hours to live. Make better use of them." But Moses bargains on furiously. "Let me live on the wrong side of the Jordan," he begs. "Let me live someplace else altogether. Let me live on as a beast of the field or a bird in the sky." "Now you have only one hour," God says. "Now you have only a few minutes."

We see the same fear of death, and the same clinging to life at all costs, among the rabbis of the Talmud. In Masechet Moed Katan we read that when Rav Seorim, Rabbi Raba's brother, was sitting by his bedside, he saw Raba drifting in and out of death. Then Raba sat up and said to him: "Please tell the Angel of Death not to torment me." Rav Seorim said: "*Me* tell him? I thought *you* were his intimate friend." Raba replied: "Since my *mazal* [fortune] has been handed over to him, he takes no heed of me." Rav Seorim then asked: "After you die, show yourself to me in a dream." Raba did this, and as soon as he appeared, Rav Seorim asked: "Did it hurt?" Raba said: "No; it was like lifting a hair out of a bowl of milk, but were the Holy One to say to me, Go back to the world as you were, I wouldn't do it. That's how great a burden the fear of death is."

The rabbis were quite full of this fear, and they used all their wit and piety to try to outwit the Angel of Death. Rabbi Eleazer was eating Trumah, the special food set aside for offerings which only the priests could eat, when the Angel of Death showed himself to him. "You can't take me while I'm performing such a great mitzvah," he told the Angel of Death, and so the fatal moment was averted. Rabbi Sheset also averted death for a few moments. He caught sight of the angel in the marketplace, and he said: "Will you seize me out in the open like a beast? Come to the house and do it." Rav Ashi also caught sight of the Angel of Death in the marketplace. He said, "Give me thirty days to review my studies, for isn't it written, 'Happy is he that comes here bringing his learning ready with him'?" The Angel of Death came again on the thirtieth day. "What's the hurry?" Ashi asked. Death replied, "Your successor, Huna Ben Natan, is close on your heels."

As for Hisda, the Angel of Death could never overcome him, because he would never shut up. He was always repeating Torah out loud. So the angel settled on a cedar tree outside the house of study. The tree cracked, Rav Hisda was distracted and stopped studying out loud for a moment, and the angel overcame him.

As for Rabbi Hiya, he was so busy that the Angel of Death couldn't get an appointment to see him. (Apparently, we are not the first to believe that workaholism will save us from the Angel of Death.) So one day the angel adopted the disguise of a poor man and rapped at the gate, saying, "Bring me out some bread." This Rabbi Hiya couldn't resist, so he opened the door to him, whereupon the angel showed him a fiery sword and made him yield his soul.

All the world is a narrow bridge, and the essential thing is not to be afraid, Rebbe Nachman said. But the fear persists, nonetheless. Marlene Adler Marks writes:

Our modern world is notoriously uncomfortable about death. Not for us the washing of the body, the sitting with the corpse, the acknowledgment that this end will be ours. All we've done is suppress the truth. I prefer the Hasidic way, and the tales that give death the power and the majesty that it is due. Here, for example, is the 19th-century story of Rabbi Loew, who tried to subvert the Angel of Death. One day near Yom Kippur, the Angel of Death came into Rabbi Loew's town. He carried with him a long scroll on which was inscribed the names of all those members of the synagogue who were to die by plague in the coming year. The Rabbi confronted the Angel of Death, tore the scroll from his hands, and threw the parchment into the fire. Almost every single one was saved, but one name was left on the scroll . . . it was his own.

I have been thinking about this last story a lot lately. I have been the rabbi at my present congregation for twelve years now. I've never stayed in one place for nearly this long before, and now I am beginning to understand why. A rabbi gets very close to the members of his congregation. It is, when all is said and done, an extremely tender relationship, a love relationship, a family relationship, and I say this with a full consciousness of the many tensions and imperfections on both sides of the metaphor. In any case, when I first came here, there was a whole generation of congregants in their late sixties, seventies, and early eighties. I have buried many of these people over the past twelve years. What is worse, I have watched many of the rest grow frail and vulnerable. I have watched their skin turn pale, and their spines curve, and their hearing desert them. I have seen them through strokes and depressions. Not a day goes by on this job that I don't think of that cry of the heart we utter so unexpectedly during the Shemah Kolenu (Hear Our Voices) prayer: "Don't abandon us, God, in our old age!" a cry that rises up from us precisely because we do feel abandoned then; abandoned by God, abandoned by our community, abandoned by our bodies.

The other day I did a funeral for one of these people, and there were many elderly there, shoveling dirt onto the coffin. Afterward a younger relative said to me, "I couldn't help thinking how they must have felt — how they must have thought, Soon it will be me." Her words went through me like a knife, because this is what I have been thinking more and more lately. More and more, I have lost my immunity to the fear of death. More and more, as I watch people I have come to love very deeply growing weak, bending over as if reaching for the grave, and then actually dying, I feel the dirt in the grave falling on me. And like Moses and the rabbis, I find myself begging for life. I feel the fear of death intensely. I feel how even the very worst days of my life, those days when I lie there depressed and exhausted with the TV blaring mindlessly on the other side of the room — I feel how even those days are infinitely rich and infinitely precious, and I pray to God not to take them away, and I pray for the strength to make better use of them.

—

And I felt this same feeling that day in the intensive care nursery with this perfect infant traveling so rapidly between birth and death, traversing that bridge so quickly. I looked around and tried to imagine what it must be like for his family. And I thought how we all begin this journey with a particular crew — with our primal family. Then little by little, one by one, we are separated from them. One goes off to Chicago to marry. Another is carried away by business. Another disappears into the darkness, the darkness that awaits us all, and then there we are on the bridge alone.

And in a flash of time, before we can say what has happened to us, a rabbi is reciting the Vidui over our prostrate form. We are too weak to say it ourselves, already engulfed by the darkness into which we are slipping, so that the rabbi's words come to us as if through deep water, and suddenly we remember hearing his words through another watery confusion, another sea — the sea of our chaotic infant consciousness.

We are in a synagogue, being held against our father's shoulders in a pink blanket, hearing the rabbi say our real name for the first time. Or we are home. The room is full of the babble of strangers. A man is standing over us with a knife. He puts a piece of cotton daubed with wine into our mouth and we suck like crazy. It's very sweet and reassuring, but then we see the horror in our mother's face and we feel the cold steel against our most intimate flesh and we begin to scream. There is nothing behind us, and nothing ahead except this narrow bridge, and beyond that only a great wind, that same wind the psalmist saw, that wind that will come by the moment after we have withered away like the grass, when no one will even be able to see the place where we were.

Suddenly we understand why the Great Temple of Jerusalem was an elaborate construction surrounding nothing. There at the sacred center, at the Holy of Holies, a place we only entered on Yom Kippur, and even then only by proxy, only through the agency of the high priest, there at that center, is precisely nothing — a vacated space, a charged emptiness, mirroring the charged emptiness that surrounds this world, that comes before this life and after it as well. Now we understand the deep wisdom of the poet Robinson Jeffers, who wrote:

> To labor eighty years in a notch of eternity is nothing too
>   tiresome,
> Enormous repose after, enormous repose before, the flash of
>   activity.
> Surely you never have dreamed the incredible depths were
>   prologue and epilogue merely
> To the surface play in the sun, the instant of life, what is
>   called life? I fancy
> That silence is the thing, this noise a found word for it;
>   interjection, a jump of the breath at that silence;
> Stars burn, grass grows, men breathe: as a man finding
>   treasure says "Ah!" but the treasure's the essence;
> Before the man spoke it was there, and after he has spoken
>   he gathers it, inexhaustible treasure.

Now we understand Moses, pleading for life with all his heart at the beginning of Parshat Vayelech, and then, when he finally lets go, when he finally accepts that he has to die, when he finally surrenders, we understand why he turns around and says, Well then, read my Torah every seven years at Sukkot. Read the record of my spiritual heritage. Read what arose out of the charged emptiness at the center of my being.

Now we understand why the rabbis said, Repent one day before your death. Which, of course, could be today.

And we understand as well why we rehearse our death on Yom Kippur — why we say Vidui and wear a kittel and refrain from eating — why in the middle of this day, we send our proxy, now the cantor, into the dangerous emptiness at our center.

We need a taste of this emptiness, to give us a sense of what will go with us, what will endure as we make this great crossing. What's important? What is at the core of our life? What will live on after we are wind and space? What will be worthy of that endless, infinitely powerful silence? And what are we clinging to that isn't important, that won't endure, that isn't worthy?

What do we want to live on? Our money, our pride? Our anger, our selfishness? If not, we better let go of them now, before they become what we are, what we will always be in that great emptiness for which we are bound.

What lives on of the people we have loved and lost? What breaks our hearts when we think of them? What do we miss so much that it aches? Precisely that suchness, that unspeakable, ineffable, intangible quality, which takes up no space at all and which never did.

That's what survives that great crossing with us. That's what makes it through the passage from life to death. And we taste death on Yom Kippur to remind us of what we must hold on to, and what we must let go of, of who we are, and where we come from.

—

We taste death on Yom Kippur to remind us that death forgives, and that Yom Kippur is a little death, and that they both cover over, like the snow that falls at the end of James Joyce's story "The Dead."

It was falling on every part of the dark central plain, on the treeless hills, falling softly upon the Bog of Allen and, farther westward, softly falling into the dark mutinous Shannon waves. It was falling, too, upon every part of the lonely churchyard. . . . It lay thickly drifted on the crooked . . . headstones, on the spears of the little gate, on the barren thorns. His soul swooned slowly as he heard the snow falling faintly through the universe and faintly falling, like the descent of their last end, upon all the living and the dead.

Turn One Day Before Your Death

One of the ironies of Jewish-American life is that Yom Kippur often takes place against the backdrop of either the baseball playoffs or the World Series itself.

In 1986 I had a congregation full of Mets fans, in the suburbs of New York. The Mets were locked in a tense playoff with the Houston Astros, and a critical game fell on the night of Kol Nidre. We had half our usual attendance for Kol Nidre that night. It was then that I realized that baseball and Yom Kippur were competing religions.

Baseball is a religion of winning. We identify with a team, and when they win we feel a lift — we feel as if we have won. When they lose, we just don't pay very close attention. Even fans of perennial losers (a religion in itself) or those rare and true fans who appreciate loss for the depth of feeling it provokes, and for the wellsprings of compassion and affection it opens, begin with a yearning to win. Otherwise there would be nothing to lose in the first place.

Yom Kippur, on the other hand, is all about losing. Losing nobly, perhaps, but losing nevertheless.

As our friends the Buddhists cheerfully remind us, suffering is inevitable in life. It is, in fact, life's first noble truth. Suffering is endemic to the experience of being alive, and Yom Kippur is the day when we Jews also acknowledge the truth of this. We acknowledge that we have fallen short, and we acknowledge that life has fallen short of our expectations as well.

Life is a series of crushing disappointments. As Kurt Vonnegut once said, "Maturity is a bitter disappointment for which no remedy exists." And the fact is that as life progresses, most of us find ourselves living our lives among the mounting debris of shattered hope. There is a certain point in our lives when it becomes clear that we are not going to attain what we dreamed of attaining in our lives, or far worse, we do attain it and it isn't what we thought it would be.

We suffer broken relationships with our parents or our children. A close friendship goes bad or simply withers from distance and neglect.

We suffer the death of those who are close to us and the diminishment of our own capacities through illness or through the simple advancement of time and of age.

Winning? Come on. How can we talk about winning when the overwhelming first-person biological reality of our experience as human beings is that from our twenties forward, we are unmistakably, definitively losing?

Except, of course, for one small detail. There is in fact one human capacity that actually increases, that grows stronger and deeper as we grow older, and that is wisdom. And the reason wisdom increases as we age is that the source of all wisdom is precisely our death. As we approach death, we approach wisdom.

We see this in the Torah with Moses, at the moment before his death. We often read this passage just before Yom Kippur. With his death upon him, Moses is no longer afraid of it, and he has a vision beyond his own life. At the moment of death, the Torah suggests, we finally stop denying death, and when this happens, we also stop denying life. We finally see our lives for what they really are.

Jacob is an even better example. His son Joseph comes to visit him as he lies dying, and he summons up his last jot of strength and tells Joseph two things. "God almighty appeared to me at Luz in the land of Canaan and blessed me," he says, and a little later he continues, "And as for me, Rachel died on me, along the way, in the land of Canaan." Standing at the last moment of his life, Jacob is able to see it clearly, and to express its meaning with great precision. The most significant moment for Jacob spiritually was the first time God appeared to him at Luz, which he then renamed Beth El (the House of God) in honor of the experience. This was the event, it was now clear to him, that had shaped his life, that had given him his mission. Personally, emotionally ("as for me"), the most significant event in his life, he could now see, was the death of his beloved wife Rachel, whom he had to bury along the side of the road near Efrat.

—

In my years as a hospice chaplain I often witnessed this kind of vision. As death approached, even the most ordinary people often acquire the ability to sum up the truth of their lives, often in a single heartbreaking sentence. "I married the wrong man, and I lived without love all my life," one woman told me during the last hours of her life. "I never wrote that book I always meant to write," a dying man told me. "This life was a precious opportunity and I squandered it."

And at the moment of our own death, we also become capable of blessing, of seeing deeply into those we love, and giving to them from the core of our being. The deathbed blessing is a commonplace in the Torah. Isaac blesses Jacob and Esau. Moses and Jacob bless all their sons. They are able to do so because the proximity of death opens their eyes. Suddenly they can see all the way to the core of their own essential nature and pass on the full force of their spiritual burden from there.

I began to admire Mayor Giuliani of New York City about a year and a half before the events of 9/11 cast him in such a heroic light. I had never liked him much, but I began to change my mind about him during the period when he was trying to decide whether or not to run for the United States Senate. In the end, he decided not to run. Things had not been going well for him. First there were the reports of his marital infidelity. Then came the news that he had prostate cancer and was in need of immediate treatment. Finally he held a press conference to announce that he was withdrawing from the race. This is what he said:

I have had a hard time deciding whether to run or not and deciding what kind of treatment to choose. This has never happened to me before. Until now, I have always been able to make difficult decisions when I had to. But this time I have found in thinking about it, in suffering over it, that something that is very painful and very difficult, but also very beautiful happens to you. It makes you figure out what you're really all about and what's really important to you. It makes you figure out what should be important to you, and where the core of you really exists. I guess, because I've been in politics so long, I used to think the core of me was politics, but perhaps it isn't.

Giuliani had always struck me as a tough, hard-charging sort of figure before this. Perhaps that was why I didn't like him very much. But here he was in his midfifties, hesitating magnificently. All of a sudden the possibility of death loomed before him and forced him to take a long, hard look at himself, to ask himself the most fundamental kind of questions. Who am I? What is my life really about?

We Jews aren't supposed to wait for the end before we ask ourselves those questions. We are supposed to ask them all the time, and especially on Yom Kippur. Yom Kippur urges us to ask them over and over again. The tradition urges us to ask them. Turn one day before your death, Rabbi Yehudah Ha Nasi tells us in the Talmud, and we never know when that day might be, so we have to turn every day. And Rabbi Jack Riemer reminds us we are not supposed to wait for a hanging, or for the doctors to pronounce that awesome word of judgment "malignant," because by then it might be too late. We are supposed to ask these questions all the time, and at least once a year, at least on this solemn day. What is my life really about? What is the truth of my life?

This is why Yom Kippur is a rehearsal for our death, the day we wear a shroud and abstain from all life-affirming activities. The day we intone the funereal liturgy "Who will live and who will die?" The rabbis wanted to bring us to the point of existential crisis. They wanted to bring us to the point of asking the crucial question, What is my life all about? And they knew, as Rabbi Yehudah Ha Nasi and Mayor Giuliani knew, that few of us ask this question until it's too late; few of us ask this question until the last moments of our life. So they have us stage a dramatic re-creation of our death on this day.

For my entire lifetime, the economic climate has been such that it has been fairly easy for most of us to feel as if we've been winning. But the truth is, no one wins this game. No one gets out of this one alive. The best we can do is to lose nobly, and to lose nobly means to be able to say at the end of our days that we know what our life is about. We know what's at its core. To lose nobly means to answer that question in time to move toward that core while we are still alive.

The irony is, it is precisely losing, it is precisely failure and loss and death, that seem to push us to the point of finally asking this question.

I know a married couple who went through a major crisis. She had an affair. He was crushed and angry, of course, and the marriage seemed doomed. But as we spoke in my office, it developed that the affair was not the problem; it was merely the symptom of the problem. The problem was that the couple had fallen into a crushing deadness in their marriage. They had become careless about spending time together and rarely did, except to collapse in a stupor every evening after both of them got home from their very demanding jobs, comatose and half dead, before the TV.

The affair was a failure, a horrible, unconscious act of anger, as adultery usually is. I don't recommend it. But the truth is, it also brought them back to life. The affair might have been the beginning of the end of their marriage, or it might have been the beginning of the renewal of their marriage, but the point is, it woke them up. It brought them back to the core of their being, that pulsing center of their lives from which they were estranged.

The proximity of death, the ultimate failure, also seems to open us this way. In his novel *The Idiot*, Fyodor Dostoyevsky wrote a thinly veiled account of the time the czar played a terrible joke on Dostoyevsky and his circle of revolutionary intellectual friends. The czar had them all arrested. And then one morning they were awakened at dawn and told they were to be executed. As Dostoyevsky rode to the execution with his friends in an open wagon, a strange sensation began to overcome him. He felt a spacious, oceanic sense of time. He felt as if the limits of time had opened wide. In a few minutes he would die, but he felt as if he had all the time in the world to do what he needed to do. What he needed to do, he now realized, was to say good-bye to his comrades for the final time. He did this in a full and leisurely way, the great love he bore his comrades welling up to the bursting point. Then he decided to spend his last moments on earth looking around at the world for the last time. As he did so, he found himself gazing at the tin roof of a nearby barn. A brilliant morning sun was shining, and a great burst of sunlight shone off the tin roof. Suddenly Dostoyevsky knew for a certainty that was what he would become. In a few minutes he would die, and he would become this blazing, radiant light. This knowledge filled him with an ecstasy so intense he thought that if it went on for even another minute, he wouldn't be able to bear it. It was then that the czar's captain told them it was all a joke. The czar had only wanted to frighten them. They wouldn't die after all. Dostoyevsky was changed forever by this experience. It showed him what he was. It took him to the core of his being, and he was a different man for the rest of his life.

This is what Yom Kippur asks us today. What is the core of our life? Are we living by it? Are we moving toward it?

We shouldn't wait until the moment of our death to seek the answers. At the moment of death, there may be nothing we can do about it but feel regret. But if we seek the answers now, we can act in the coming year to bring ourselves closer to our core. This is the only life we have, and we all will lose it. No one gets out alive, but to lose nobly is a beautiful thing. To know the core of our being is to move beyond winning and losing.

It is to enter that moment where life is deep and rich and God is present for us. We all lose, some of us nobly, and all of us with a certain amount of tragedy. But as Rabbi Zimmerman (a.k.a. Bob Dylan) reminds us, "there's no success like failure," and any loss that carries us closer to the core of life is no loss at all.

Selichah/Forgiveness

Rabbi Shlomo Carlebach, the legendary spiritual leader and composer of Jewish music, came to the United States from Austria as a teenager, a refugee from the Nazis. Every so often he would go back to Austria and Germany to give concerts, and people would ask him, "How can you go back there and give concerts? Don't you hate them after what they did to you? Don't you hate the Austrians and the Germans?"

And this is what Shlomo would say to anyone who asked him this question: "I only have one soul. If I had two souls, I would gladly devote one of them to hating the Germans full-time. But I don't. I only have one soul, and I'm not going to waste it on hating."

Every year we meet for Yom Kippur in the pall of death, not only because the Yom Kippur liturgy is so full of death, but also because it is quite striking when people die at this time. People die of course at all times, but when they die during the High Holidays as we are intoning the solemn liturgy "Who will live and who will die?" their deaths make more of an impression than usual.

But one year the pall of death was particularly heavy. Many people from my synagogue had died during and just before the holidays, and my cantor's father lay on the brink of death as well. This cantor was a very young man, at least he had been when he first came to work with me. I used to like to tease him about it. It says in the Shulchan Aruch, the great compendium of Jewish law, that the cantor who leads the congregation in prayer during the High Holidays must be at least thirty years old, and that he must be married and have many children and an empty cupboard, so that when he prays on behalf of the congregation he will pray with a broken heart.

And I would tease the cantor, because when he first came here, he was still in his twenties and he was single and childless, and he seemed never to have experienced a moment of significant suffering in his entire life. Then the next year he was married, and the year after that, he had a child, and then he had another child, and then he turned thirty. And this particular year, at Selichot services on the Saturday night before Rosh Hashanah, his heart broke in two, right in the middle of the service.

His father was dying then; he would actually die around twenty-five hours later. The cantor and his father had been extremely close. The cantor had three sisters and no brothers, so he and his father had been the only males in the house, and they had a very deep and a very tender bond. The cantor had even chosen to follow in his father's career — he was only a part-time cantor. His father had been an eminent statistician, and the cantor had followed him into this field. At Selichot the cantor was literally sick with concern for his father. He hadn't slept for some time. His voice was cracking, and he was emotionally distraught. And sitting right behind him, I could feel how deeply the words of the Selichot service were affecting him. But when he got to the Shemah Kolenu (Hear Our Voices) prayer, it just became too much for him.

Hear our voice; please listen to us, Lord our God; do not cast us out from your presence. Do not take your Holy Spirit from us. When our strength has ebbed away, don't abandon us. This is the line that really got to the cantor, I think. His father had been a brilliant mathematician — one of the leading statisticians of his generation — and in the past few days he had been losing his mental faculties. The cantor had called him that day and he had been speaking gibberish. So when he started chanting that line — When our strength has ebbed away, don't abandon us — that's when he lost it. That's when he started sobbing on the altar.

—

And when the service was over, he said to me, "You know, every year we say those words without having any idea what they mean. What are we thinking of? What do we think we're doing?"

So that year at our High Holiday services there was even more than the usual sense of how tenuous life is; more than the usual sense of what an ephemeral and precious gift this soul of ours is

We only have one soul. Why do we waste it on hatred? Why do we find it so difficult to forgive? What are we thinking of?

The rabbis of the Talmud used to go to great lengths to make themselves available to grant forgiveness to the people who had wronged them. They felt they couldn't offer forgiveness until it was requested, because they were afraid to short-circuit the inner process of Teshuvah. They understood that in order for forgiveness to be complete, the person who had wronged them needed to arrive at the point of a sincere apology by his or her own inner process, and they didn't want to interfere with this process. So if someone owed them an apology, they would hover around him constantly, both to remind him of what he had done and to be on hand to grant forgiveness the moment the person apologized. The rabbis recognized that forgiveness was a deep spiritual need for both parties. The wrongdoer needed to be cleansed of his wrongdoing and his guilt for it, and his victim needed to let go of the hot coal of anger he was holding on to. So the rabbis hovered around the people who had wronged them, so that both these needs could be met at the earliest possible moment.

I have a friend named Frank Osteseski who is the director of a local hospice. One of his patients was an elderly woman, a simple, country kind of person. One day, not too long before she died, her brother showed up at the hospice. Her brother was a cowboy. He worked in the rodeo, traveling from town to town, and he came in wearing a big Stetson hat and a belt buckle the size of a football. He hadn't seen his sister, it turned out, for twenty or thirty years. Obviously they weren't close. But he stayed at the hospice with her for several weeks. Their attempts at conversation were painful to listen to and never amounted to more than the merest small talk. The rest of the time he just kind of hung out, sitting in the courtyard smoking cigarettes and trying to stay out of people's way.

One evening Frank was just getting ready to leave the hospice — walking out the door in fact — when suddenly the cowboy came up to him and said, "Well, I guess I got to say it sooner or later," and Frank said to himself, Well, I better sit down, because I'm not going to be leaving here anytime soon.

Thus began a long conversation, in which little by little and in fits and starts this cowboy told Frank the true story of his life and his sister's life as well. They had been quite poor as small children — dirt poor in fact — and after their mother died, their father neglected them, abused them, and then finally abandoned them altogether. They had been placed in foster homes, one nightmare after another. And during those years, he had been mean to his sister — very mean. In fact he had abused her and hurt her very badly, and when they grew up, they drifted apart and became estranged from each other. Now that she was dying, he felt terrible about it. After this conversation, Frank took him into his sister's room and stood by him while he asked her for forgiveness. He told her that he realized that he had treated her very badly and that he was very, very sorry, and he begged her to forgive him.

—

His sister was quiet for a while, and then, speaking with great difficulty, as she was very close to death, she said, "The people here feed me. The people here keep me clean. I'm surrounded with love. I have everything I need. There's no blame."

When this big tough cowboy with the Stetson hat and the belt buckle as big as a football heard these words, he dissolved. His face was consumed first with an infinite sadness, then with wonder and amazement, until finally it looked like the face of an innocent child. He was transformed by his sister's forgiveness. In a moment, in an instant, he had been relieved of a lifetime's pain. There's no blame, his sister said, because she was surrounded by love and had everything she needed, and she understood very well that she would only imprison herself if she continued to harbor anger and resentment toward her brother. She understood that anger can never produce love. Only love can produce love. Only compassion can free us from the prison of our own anger, the compassion we feel for others, and the compassion we feel from them, and the compassion we feel for ourselves.

And it took a great deal for her to be able to understand all that. It took the love, the sense of having her needs provided for. But also, I think, it took the fact that she knew she was dying and needed to free her soul from its earthly binds; I don't think she could have let go without this. Letting go of our anger and the leverage we imagine it gives us against others is one of the hardest things a human being can do.

Who will live and who will die? None of us knows what will happen this year. Most of us will live, but some of us in fact will die, and it might be me and it might be you. But whether we live or we die, we will only have one soul to do it with, one precious soul to inhabit for our brief moment on this mortal coil. Why have we chosen to torment this soul, to fill it with anger and hatred, to hold on to the hot coal of self-righteousness with all our might, in the foolish hope that it may someday hurt the person we imagine to be our enemy, while all the while, it's only hurting us, while all the while it is our own soul — the only soul we have — that is writhing in torment.

What have we been thinking of?

KAPARAH/ATONEMENT

Yom Kippur, or the day of kaparah, the Day of Atonement, is about the purification of the soul. The language of the soul is paradox. Rabbi Akiva spoke this language in a famous aphorism found in Pirke Avot. "All is foreseen and free will is in our hands," Rabbi Akiva said. Every moment of life is the inevitable consequence of everything that has ever happened since the universe exploded into being. At the same time, we are absolutely free to respond to this inevitability, and our response will also become part of the inevitable flow of the universe. Yom Kippur begins with the Kol Nidre service, and Kol Nidre is a ritual for the nullification of vows. There is a time in life, for many of us, where the idea of the nullification of a vow is very real indeed. I am speaking about divorce. Jewish divorce is a spiritual act, and it should be no surprise, then, that this ritual also rests on a paradox. When a Jewish marriage fails, a religious divorce is absolutely necessary. The very powerful spiritual act we performed under the chuppah, the marriage canopy — that profound alteration of the universe — must be undone. Yet at the same time it cannot be undone. Love is as strong as death, and marriage, if it contains even the slightest trace of love, lasts forever. Its consequences reverberate until the end of time. So when a marriage fails, we must divorce, in order to undo that which cannot possibly be undone.

My own first wedding ceremony took place in a small Orthodox synagogue in Atlanta, Georgia. I was twenty-two years old. The pews were all full, and all my grandparents, now long since dead, were smiling up at me from the front row. Two rabbis presided, the rabbi of the synagogue, and the ninety-nine-year-old rabbi emeritus, who had married my intended's parents. By this time the old rabbi was quite feeble — quite frail — and his role in the ceremony was confined to the reading of the Ketuvah, the wedding contract. As this was an Orthodox synagogue, he was to read the entire Ketuvah, a very long document, in the original Aramaic. A few minutes into the recitation, this ancient rabbi suddenly and inexplicably fell silent. The pause grew longer, and then longer and longer and longer. First discomfort and then a palpable ripple of alarm began to pass through the assembly. I looked up at the old man. He seemed to have left this plane of existence altogether. His eyes were rolled back into his skull, and his face seemed blank, empty, uninhabited by a spirit. Where had he gone? What should we do about it? No one seemed to know. The old rabbi was a figure of such veneration that no one would dare so much as jostle his arm or suggest that he get on with the Ketuvah reading in some other way. Nor did anyone wish to acknowledge the horrifying possibility that a full-blown crisis might be in progress — that the rabbi might have suddenly suffered a stroke, or lost his marbles, or, for all we could tell, even died standing up, right in the middle of the wedding.

So we all just stood there for a long time — a measureless time out of time, an unbearably long time. Then, as abruptly as he had stopped, the rabbi started up again, picking up exactly where he had left off in the Aramaic text, without the slightest acknowledgment that anything out of the ordinary had happened.

Everyone was quite relieved. I broke the glass, the dancing began, but eventually the marriage failed. Not as a result of this strange gap in the proceedings. No, I am quite sure it was the other way around. I am quite sure that there must have been some invisible flaw in the marriage which had sent the old rabbi spinning off prematurely to the next world. Over the course of time, this flaw simply made itself manifest in this dimension as well.

I was still in my twenties when this flaw became so pronounced that we realized we could no longer stay together. The marriage had actually been failing for many years, but we were having a hard time finally breaking apart. We were in torment. We separated several times and then came back together again. We got a civil divorce, but that didn't seem to work either. We continued to go back and forth. We were paralyzed, our lives were on hold. True, we had a child together, and we both loved him very much, and that certainly made the separation more difficult. But there was more to it than that.

Then one morning I woke up to a vision: I saw the old rabbi before me again, his eyes blank and rolled back, his soul off in another dimension. Then I felt precisely what it had felt like under that chuppah; it was an extraordinary feeling, a powerful feeling, the very soul of ambivalence itself.

Suddenly both the problem of my life and its solution were unmistakably clear: we had never undone the spiritual bond we had created under the chuppah. We had undone the legal bond, but that had never been our problem. Our problem was on the spiritual plane. Now we would have to get a Jewish divorce — a *get*. I called my first wife right away. "Of course," she said. "That's it!" So we set about to get a Jewish divorce, and our marriage finally ended. We had been living apart, but we were finally able to separate on the spiritual level. The spiritual bond between us was severed, and we both went about our separate lives, both marrying again, this time happily and successfully.

Except, of course, for the dreams I would continue to have about her for the rest of my life. Except, of course, for the times I call my present wife by my first wife's name. Except, of course, for the annoying fact that in a certain dimension — no doubt the same dimension the old rabbi visited during our wedding ceremony — we will always be married. When we marry, an indissoluble bond adheres. So why bother to divorce?

We may as well ask, and especially on Yom Kippur, why bother to seek atonement for our sins? Why bother to seek kaparah? In fact it is exactly the same question, namely, can the consequences of our behavior, good or bad, ever really be effaced, wiped away, swept clean? And the answer is, of course not. Every time the famous Butterfly of Uncertainty flaps its wings in China, it sets off an ineluctable chain of events — hurricanes, tornadoes, the reformation of the continents, and so on and so forth until the end of time. No action can ever be undone, nor its consequences ever effaced.

So why do we fast all day on Yom Kippur? Why do we submit ourselves to this yearly ritual of self-abnegation? Why even bother to ask anyone for forgiveness?

Kaparah, the Hebrew word for atonement, means a covering over. The idea is not that atonement effaces our sins. It cannot. They will always be there, along with everything else we and everyone else has ever done — an endless and indissoluble concatenation of cause and effect, stretching back to the beginning of time and reaching forward to its end as well. When we make atonement, kaparah, we are covering over our wrongdoing with the will to behave differently. While this does not efface our previous behavior, it may, in fact, redeem it. More important, it allows us to move on and let go of the past. Our behavior is still out there, and will always be, but we are no longer attached to it. We no longer need to feel guilty or angry about it. We no longer need to feel as if we have failed. The original act may even still adhere to us, but we no longer claim ownership of it. We have covered that over with a fresh act of will.

I try my best to be a good rabbi, but I'm working with very limited equipment and sometimes I let people down. Someone who had read my first book once told me that while they enjoyed reading it very much, they thought the book might have been too honest. They thought it really made me look like a shlimazel, that classic figure of Jewish literature who is the constant victim of bad luck and his own remedial bungling. He wondered what some congregants would think about having such a shlimazel for a rabbi. A lot of people want their rabbi to be a father, like Robert Young in *Father Knows Best,* or if not actually God, at least a stand-in for God. And I know a lot of rabbis who spend their whole life's energy pretending to be these things. I don't have that kind of energy. I try to make the best of what I have by offering up my shlimazelhood to others, in the hope that this may illuminate their own inner shlimazel and help them come to terms with it. Maybe then they won't have to spend so much of their life's energy defending against the truth of their own lives. But I am a shlimazel, and sometimes I let people down. Sometimes I let them down because it just can't be helped. Sometimes I just can't get to them. I find myself doing triage all the time, and sometimes I let people down because there might be a dozen more pressing concerns that stand between their need and my ability to reach them.

But sometimes I let people down because I simply blow it. I don't do what I'm supposed to do for one reason or another; or for no reason whatsoever that I am able to fathom, I just fail. And sometimes the consequences of my failure can be quite serious. There is a young couple in my congregation I like very well. I admire them. I converted the woman, and I married them several years ago. It was a beautiful wedding too, at a lovely winery up in Sonoma County, a day, like all wedding days, full of hope and fond dreams. But then they had a horrible tragedy. The child they had been expecting was born dead, and the mother had a perilous time of it herself for a while. Her husband called me a few days after this had all taken place. It so happened I had the flu at the time he called. I told him I didn't want to come to the hospital just then, because I was afraid I would make his wife sick, but I promised to come in a few days, when I was better. But you know what, I never went. I still don't know what happened. I simply don't remember. Maybe in my weakened condition I just didn't want to face such a painful situation. Or maybe there was just too much on my plate — phone calls, meetings, and people trooping in and out of my office in various states of distress — and I just couldn't keep track of it all. Or maybe my memory was failing, or maybe I really was just a callous SOB who only pretended to care about people. In any case, for one reason or another, I forgot all about this couple and their terrible tragedy.

I recovered from my flu a few days later, and the whole thing — as serious, as grave as it was — the whole thing just slipped through my mind. It just fell through the cracks, and I never even thought about it again until months later, when I learned this couple had left the synagogue in disgust — hurt and in great pain. They were devastated by my not showing up — crushed. The husband told me it was the biggest religious disappointment of his life. I called them up to apologize, and of course they accepted my apology and forgave me. They are very fine people. But believe me, this is written in the book of my life. It is written indelibly and it's sealed as well. I could ask them for forgiveness, but I couldn't ask them to undo what had happened. No one could do that. Nor could anyone undo the hurt they experienced or the disillusionment of the young woman. I had converted her to Judaism! And most significantly, from my point of view, no one could change this judgment of who I really was. "Your feet take you to where you really want to go," the young man told me when I called him to apologize, and I knew he was right. I might think of myself as a great, compassionate healer. I might think of myself as a caring, giving person, always there for people when they need me. I might tell story after story casting myself in this role, but this was the unavoidable truth of my life. This was what was written in the book of my life. This is where my feet had taken me, or more precisely, where they had failed to take me.

So why even bother to ask for forgiveness? Why make kaparah? That behavior needs to be covered over precisely because it will always be out there. Their hurt needed to be covered over. It was like an exposed wound, an open sore, and it needed to be covered over by an acknowledgment that they had been hurt, by a validation of what they had experienced, by a corroboration from me that I had hurt them. Then they could begin to heal from it, or at least from the part I was responsible for. They could then begin to let go of it. And I needed to cover this act of thoughtlessness over with a new resolve. It will always be out there; it will always be part of the story of who I am. Only a part, to be sure. There have been many occasions when I was there for people. More than once I have gotten out of bed in the middle of the night to go sit with strangers at the hospital. But that's the part of the story I like to tell. Now there's another part, a part I don't want to look at so much. Only by responding differently when this sort of thing happens in the future can I cover it over with another story, one that might change its meaning yet again.

This is why atonement is like divorce. Our marriages never leave us. They cling to us in our dreams, and in the names we call up from our unconscious. But the ritual of divorce covers them over with a fresh act of will, and this act will create a flow of consequences that covers over the old one.

—

Every once in a while, maybe just a few times in life, you can feel the force of this — the flow of consequences that has brought you to the present moment of your life. You can actually experience a moment as the product of the totality of all creation.

I had such a moment some years ago. I was visiting a man who was both mentally challenged and exceedingly small — a dwarf, in fact — in a halfway house up on Diamond Height in San Francisco. He was in immense emotional pain. Whenever we sat together he would ask me questions like, "How come God didn't let me grow? Why won't God take me?" These were questions I could never answer, of course. Then one day I was ushered into the living room of the halfway house to see him, and there he was. He had just put a Beatles record on the old phonograph they had there, and "She Came In Through the Bathroom Window" was blasting all over the house, and he was singing along at the top of his lungs and dancing across the living room floor with a heartbreaking, wholehearted passion and joy. Behind him as he danced was a great panoramic view: the bay, the Oakland hills, the downtown skyscape. And as I walked in upon this scene, the enormity of what had produced it suddenly struck me. Think of what went into this moment. Start anywhere. Start, for example, with the entire cultural history of western civilization; a culture that twisted and turned for more than two thousand years just so the Beatles could come tumbling out in the end.

Or start with the technology of the phonograph record.

Or start with the geological upheavals of the western Americas, which produced this beautiful city, these hills, this breathtaking bay.

———

Or start with the psychology and the physiology of the man himself, the immensity of his suffering and the mysterious spiritual mechanism that transformed that suffering into song and dance.

"She Came In Through the Bathroom Window."

All of it absolutely necessary, absolutely inevitable, absolutely indispensable to this explosion of pure joy — this Big Ecstatic Bang. There hasn't been enough time since the beginning of all creation for all of this to have happened by accident. This moment had been hammered into place by the totality of creation.

And stretching before us from this moment are the infinite consequences of our present action. From here, we *will* a kaparah — we let go of the pain of the past. We cover it over with a new intention, and then that intention ripples out soul to soul until it has filled all of time.

We say, "We have been married from time past until now, and that will never go away. But now I cover that over, I release you. I send you away, I put you aside."

We say, "I have sinned, I have transgressed, I have done wrong. I have done something terribly hurtful." And we say precisely what it is. We read the book we don't want to read. I have done this and I have done that, and I acknowledge it is irreversible, it can never be undone, but I cover it over now. I resolve to begin anew.

Now there is something new in the world, a new possibility. The universe is forever changed, just as we changed it under the chuppah that day when the Ancient One seemed to be elsewhere but then finally returned.

THE HAFTARAH: ISAIAH LAUGHS AT US

According to the Kabala, before creation God existed in a primordial state known alternatively as the Ain Sof (the Endlessness) and the Aiyin (the Emptiness.) But this endless emptiness was such a powerfully charged state that nothing could withstand it. Nothing could coexist in its presence. So in order to create the universe, the Ain Sof had to perform an operation known as Tzim-Tzum; it contracted itself, removing itself from a tiny speck at the center of its vast emptiness. This tiny speck was creation — the universe. But in the middle of this Tzim-Tzum — this Divine Contraction — a cosmic catastrophe occurred. The Kabalists call this catastrophe Shevirat Hakelim — the Breaking of the Vessels.

The Divine Light was being hauled away from this tiny speck at the center of the Ain Sof in vessels, but the light was too strong for the vessels and the vessels broke, and the Divine Light was scattered all over the universe, throwing the world into chaos, creating a broken and dangerous world.

The purpose of human existence, according to the Kabala, is Tikun Olam — repairing the universe, fixing the vessels, recapturing the Divine Light. Everything we can do to correct the brokenness of the world accomplishes this; spiritual activity accomplishes this, and so does the pursuit of social justice in the world.

Yet in a thoroughly broken world, when we carry our own spiritual brokenness into every endeavor, how can we expect to be the agents of real repair? How can we prevent our own brokenness from defeating every attempt we make to repair the world? Kabir, the medieval Sufi poet, writes:

I talk to my inner lover and I say, why such a rush?
We sense that there is some sort of spirit that loves birds
    and animals and the ants —
perhaps the same one who gave a radiance to you in your
    mother's womb,
Is it logical you would be walking around entirely
    orphaned now?
The truth is you turned away yourself, and decided to
    go into the dark alone.
Now you're tangled up in others and have forgotten what
    you once knew,
and that's why everything you do has some weird failure
    in it.

So according to Kabir, this weird failure, this brokenness of
the world, comes from our having turned away to enter the dark
alone.

The Haftarah (the special reading from the Prophets which
accompanies every Sabbath and festival service) we read in the
middle of the Yom Kippur service also speaks of a radiance, and a
movement from the darkness to the light. This is my favorite liturgical moment of the year. It is Yom Kippur morning and we are
feeling quite pious, quite proud of ourselves for having fasted all
the way from dinner last night to the present moment. Our growl-
ing stomach reenforces this feeling. We congratulate ourselves for
great sincerity with each fresh pang. Then all of a sudden we hear
the voice of God (through the medium of the prophet Isaiah)
mocking us, taunting us.

Is this the fast I have chosen? Is this your affliction of the
soul?
Is it to droop your head like a bullrush, to grovel in
sackcloth and ashes?
Is this what you call fasting, a fast that the Lord would
accept?
Is not this my chosen fast:
Loosen all the bonds that bind men unfairly, let the
oppressed go free, break every yoke.
Share your bread with the hungry, take the homeless into
your home.
Clothe the naked when you see him, do not turn away from
people in need.
Then cleansing light shall break forth like the dawn, and
your wounds shall soon be healed.

Isaiah is telling how we might turn away from our own darkness — from the place where everything has some weird failure to
it. When we feed the hungry, when we house the homeless, when
we care for those in need, we move toward the light.

This is advice we almost always need to hear. The stock market goes up and the stock market goes down; we feel flush and we
feel pinched. But the big picture — the overarching economic
reality of our time — is that the past sixty or seventy years have
been the longest sustained period of economic growth and the
most extensive and widespread experience of affluence in human
history. Yet we seem not one whit closer to realizing the ancient
dream of social justice and compassion. We are richer than ever,
but the gap between rich and poor has grown wider than ever at

the same time. During this time of unprecedented economic expansion, both poverty and homelessness have increased exponentially. Wealth has not trickled down. Those on the lowest economic levels have not been lifted up by the flood tides of economic growth.

The other day I was walking across a park on my way to work when a man my age came out of the bushes right in my path. We frightened each other. He recoiled from me. I realized he was afraid to be discovered. Why was he so afraid of this? Maybe it was because the city was in the middle of one of its periodic campaigns to round up the homeless and get them off the streets. But as we continued recoiling from each other in a strange kind of dance — he taking two steps back from me, me taking two steps back from him — I felt something deeper in his fear. I felt it was the nature of his state. He represented a part of us that doesn't want to be discovered. He represented a part of me that I didn't want to see; the dirty part, the uncontrollable part, the part that might fall into the black hole of failure at any moment, the part that might go belly up and die.

He was a perfect picture of everything in life that frightened me to death, of everything I couldn't control, of all my own internal monsters: death, failure, uncleanliness, and all the uncontrollable impulses — anger, lust, jealousy, and greed — these demons unleashed. No wonder I didn't want to look at him. No wonder I felt a wave of relief pass over me as he disappeared back into the bushes.

But as soon as this wave passed, I felt something else as well. I felt how much fear there was in my reluctance to see this man.

Precisely because we have such a strong sense of our own brokenness deep down, whatever happiness we experience carries a subtle undercurrent of fear. When things are going well, when we are experiencing pleasure and are getting what we want, we feel obliged to defend our happiness, because it seems so fragile, so unstable. So it is, Sharon Salzberg reminds us, that we deny the very possibility of suffering: we cut ourselves off from facing it in ourselves and in others, because we intuit our brokenness, and we fear that if we admit any kind of suffering, it will undermine or destroy our good fortune. So in order to hold on to our pleasure, we refuse to recognize the humanity of a homeless person on the street. We block out the suffering of others. We cut ourselves off from the world's suffering, because we fear it will undermine or destroy our own happiness.

But if there are homeless on our streets, we can't be happy. They accuse us. They threaten us. Even if we manage to get them out of our parks and off the downtown streets, how can we enjoy what we have if there are people begging for food and for work on the parkway dividers and in the doorways of our churches and synagogues?

The only way we can keep them from spoiling our happiness is to try to pretend that they don't exist. But whenever we try to pretend something doesn't exist, our world is reduced and we become unhappy. Happiness is precisely our experience of the fullness of the world.

I saw a film once that conveyed this sense of fullness and connection quite vividly. It was a television film about human conception made by Scandinavian scientists with microscopic cameras. At the beginning of the film, we see thousands of sperm cells pouring into the female reproductive system like the Allies storming the Normandy coast. Each cell is supremely confident of his mission in life. Each one is convinced he will triumph in the end; then one by one they flame out and die. They crash into the fallopian walls and perish, or they simply run out of steam and begin to disintegrate.

And if, right after crashing into the wall or running out of steam, one of these fallen cells were interviewed by Howard Cosell and asked what the meaning of it all might be, he would probably say, "There is no meaning to it! The whole thing is a meaningless crapshoot. You think you're going to produce a life, but then you just crash into a wall and die for no reason."

From the limited point of view of each individual cell, there is in fact no meaning to the life they have lived. Their lives seem to have been wasted and absurd. But as this magnificent film unfolds, we see that they are part of a larger process — the propagation of life itself. One single cell, against astronomical odds, penetrates the skin of the egg, and then the egg starts to revolve and send out filaments of tissue all around its circumference, so that it looks like a great sun, a great, radiant light, turning and turning in its firmament. And out of this dazzling cosmic dance comes life itself.

I felt this same sense of fullness — of being connected to a larger source of meaning and purpose — on the floor of a redwood forest once. It was toward the end of a long hike in Mendocino County, and I had just dropped down to the ground to rest in the middle of a redwood grove. There was a small branch sticking out of the ground in front of me. I reached out to pull myself up with it, but it gave way in my hand. The bottom of the living branch had already become part of the thick, rich loam that lay beneath the forest floor. I lay back and looked up through the branches crowding around me, up to the dazzling gold light at the top of the trees.

Everything was reaching for the sun; every tree, every limb, every shrub. Everything was aspiring upward toward the light and would continue to do so until it died and fell back to the forest floor. Then Divine Intelligence, embodied in a seed cone, would begin to push all this dead matter upward again in the form of new life. The forest was a single purposeful organism, and every one of its cells, living and dead, was part of this exquisite reach for the light.

We can't control sickness, old age, or death. We are terrified of them. But as Sharon Salzberg asks, what would we fear if we experienced ourselves to be part of the whole of nature, moving and changing, being born and dying? What would we fear if we understood that our bodies were joined with the planet in a continual, rhythmic exchange of matter and energy?

We do not live as isolated fragments, completely separate, but rather as parts of a great, dynamic, mutable whole. Every moment, we are dying and being reborn, we and all of life.

As individuals we live and die, often without apparent meaning. As a whole people, we are always moving toward the light.

And this sense of wholeness is precisely the healing we need, the Tikun, the repair we need to offset our sense of brokenness. Yom Kippur is a day of healing, a day of repair, a day that recognizes our fundamental brokenness and provides us with a remedy — at-one-ment, kaparah. *Kaper* means to cover. We are covered over by a consciousness of God, which blurs the imaginary distinctions we have made between ourselves and others.

We are not the first culture in the world to intuit a sense of brokenness in human existence, nor are we the first people to celebrate a yearly ritual of atonement and judgment. In ancient Greece they had a ceremony called the *pharmakos*. In the city of

Athens, a man and woman, representing all the men and women in the city, were driven away and never permitted back in the city again. This was done to propitiate the gods for the brokenness of all the citizens of Athens. This ceremony supplanted human sacrifice, and was a step toward enlightenment. Christianity and Judaism took the process one step further. Christianity sacrificed one human being — one man who died for everyone else's brokenness for all time. No further propitiations would ever be necessary. We Jews went even further; we replaced people altogether with a goat. We read about the sacrifice of the scapegoat in the Torah on the morning of Yom Kippur.

But in case we ever imagine we have really risen above our pagan impulses, all we have to do is ask ourselves, Who are we trying to run out of town at the moment? Who is our pharmakos? Whom are we asking to propitiate for our own sense of brokenness? The list of candidates is usually quite long. I've already spoken of our reluctance to acknowledge the homeless on our streets because of the fear of our own vulnerability they provoke. This is why nearly every homeless initiative that has ever been launched in American cities has been mostly concerned with getting the homeless out of sight.

And we would like to keep the hungry, the mentally ill, and the addicted of the world out of sight as well, or at least beyond our borders. They are a pointed reminder of our greed — of our addiction to consuming, of our squandering the world's resources on meaningless consumer luxuries while elsewhere in the world people starve and die. We would rather hide the victims of this behavior behind gates and fences than face it in ourselves.

And we would rather demonize homosexuals than admit to our own very complicated sexuality. Freud was right. We all have every conceivable sexual tendency within us. But since society has placed such a negative charge on certain sexual impulses, we experience them as a darkness, a brokenness, and we feverishly try to obscure them. We try to project them out onto gays and lesbians and then to demean them, to treat them as somehow deficient.

This ongoing inner process takes on a thousand forms. Out of fear, we project our inner darkness onto others. We make demons out of them and then cast them away. Out of fear, we turn away from our own sacred center.

And this has never worked, not once, and it never will. And the reason is this.

All human beings are bearers of the divine. And when we try to drive a particular group of people away, we drive God away with them. We sever ourselves from the God who has assured us a hundred times that he/she hears the cries of the oppressed and goes where they go.

Propitiation of the gods, human sacrifice, this is not the way of Yom Kippur. The way of Yom Kippur is to accept our imperfection. This is what Yom Kippur is all about. We accept that to be human is to be imperfect, to be broken, and we realize that we don't have to project our brokenness onto someone else. We don't have to try to cast it out. We can fix it. We can repair it in the context of our own lives.

The way of Yom Kippur is to realize, like Isaiah, that we are all part of a whole, and that we move toward the light of God when we behave this way, when we care for each other, when we realize in our flesh and bones that our own happiness depends on the happiness of everyone else in the world. We can't enjoy our affluence while people are starving.

—

When we experience this sense of the world, we realize that every need in the world is our need. Nature always takes care of the next need. The forest replenishes itself, the T cells in our body strive to heal. The world is set up to heal itself. Our choice is to align ourselves with this healing or not.

Compassion heals. Loving-kindness heals. Justice heals. Meditation heals. Prayer heals. The Sabbath heals. Yom Kippur heals. All these activities reenforce each other, depend upon each other, and taken together they purify us of our delusion of separation and its attending sense of absurdity. They impart a sense of the sacred to us, an immediate sense of our connection to everyone and to everything, and the imperative for engagement with the world which flows out of this sense.

So purified, we simply take care of whatever is in front of our face. We simply answer the immediate need. It is our need.

When we are hungry we eat, and when we are tired we sleep. When someone else is hungry, we feed them. When someone else is homeless, we find shelter for them.

If we try to ignore them, we only darken our own world. Better to pick up the broken shards of our vessel and begin to piece them together again. We are all broken vessels yearning for the light.

CHAPTER TEN

THE GATES CLANG SHUT

NEILAH

TWICE A YEAR DURING THE DAYS OF THE GREAT
Temple, on Tisha B'Av and on Yom Kippur, there was a
service at the end of the day, called Neilah, or closing,
because it was performed as the Temple gates were clanging shut. We still perform this service on Yom Kippur, and
we still call it Neilah, only now it is not the closing of the
Temple gates that we are referring to, but rather the closing
of the gates of heaven.

This is generally a very well attended service. At my
synagogue, people throng to the Neilah service. Most of
them have been in synagogue all day long. Since far more
people come to our Yom Kippur services than we can
accommodate in a single sanctuary sitting, we have many

services going on at once all day long. We have staggered services, alternative services, parallel services out in the social hall, several seatings in the main sanctuary. But by the afternoon service, all the people begin to trickle into the main sanctuary at once. The seats fill up quickly, then people start sitting on the floor in the aisles. People stand at the back of the room. People sit on the steps up in the balcony and pack themselves into the foyer just outside the sanctuary. As Neilah begins, I look out over a sea of faces tightly pressed together. The sanctuary is filled to more than double its capacity. I always feel a thrill of fear at this moment. Our synagogue is very old, and the main sanctuary is up on the second floor. What if the floor should collapse from the weight of all this overload? What if an earthquake were suddenly to hit? What makes these thousands of people so desperately want to crowd into a space meant to hold only a fraction of that number?

The Hasidic master Levi Yitzchak of Berditchev said that it isn't just that the gates of heaven are open during the Ten Days of Teshuvah; what is far more significant is that an energy, an attractive force, passes through this opening during these days. This is a very subtle energy, and for most of the Ten Days, when the gates are wide open, we don't even notice it. But during the Neilah service, as the gates begin to close and the opening becomes narrower and narrower, this attractive energy becomes more and more intense, more and more noticeable. It is precisely this energy which draws us to the Neilah service so intensely, and which inspires us to pray so fervently once there. The prayer we utter at Neilah is that most urgent of all human prayers, the prayer of the last chance. The gates of heaven are closing. We only have a few minutes left.

—

Looking out at the vast throng assembled before me for the Neilah service, I see a purity in these faces I never see at any other time, an innocent suspension of disbelief, a wholehearted yearning one ordinarily only sees in children.

This same Levi Yitzchak of Berditchev was famous for his chutzpah, his audacity. It was he who once put God on trial for failing to prevent the persecution and economic deprivation of the Jews of his day. Levi Yitzchak of Berditchev convicted God at this trial. He found God guilty of all charges.

One year at Neilah, Levi Yitzchak of Berditchev declared war on God, but only as a last resort. I heard this story from Rabbi Abraham Karp of Boston. Levi Yitzchak mounted the pulpit to begin the Neilah service in fear and trembling. He was absolutely determined that before the gates of heaven closed he would wrest a promise from God to give his people a year of blessing and happiness instead of the terrible suffering they had been enduring in recent years. So he did three things.

First he tried supplication. He pleaded with God. He said, "Look, God, an ordinary person who drops a treasure on the floor will stoop down and pick it up without even thinking about it. But you, dear God, you have called us your treasure, and yet you let us fall from your hands to the earth and you don't pick us up. For two thousand years, you have let us grovel in the dust of exile and you haven't bent down to pick us up. Is it too much to ask you to act like an ordinary person acts?" Levi saw his words rise up toward heaven in visible waves, and the gates of heaven stopped closing and actually began to open, but just a little bit.

So Levi Yitzchak of Berditchev decided to throw all his energy into the Vidui, the formal prayer of confession that is a standard feature of all Yom Kippur services, including Neilah. If pleading opened the gates of heaven a little bit, he thought, perhaps repentance would open them up the rest of the way. So when it came time to recite the confessional, he began to weep, and he cried out, "Woe to us. We live in a crazy world. It used to be that people told the truth on the streets and lied when they came to synagogue. Since they conducted their business in honesty and truth, when they came to synagogue and recited the Vidui on Yom Kippur and they said, 'We have sinned,' they were lying. But now the opposite is the case. They lie on the streets and they tell the truth in the synagogue. They cheat and steal in their ordinary lives, and when they come to synagogue and confess that they have sinned, they are telling the truth." A bitter cry of remorse and repentance could be heard throughout the synagogue as he concluded his Vidui. Levi Yitzchak saw the cry rising toward heaven, and it opened the gates of heaven a little bit wider, but not very far.

So Levi Yitzchak declared war on God. That was the only course left to him. Now a zaddik, a righteous saint like Levi Yitzchak of Berditchev, doesn't wage war the way a king or a general would wage war, and he doesn't use the same weapons either. A zaddik employs an army of the righteous, and their weapons are their good deeds. So in his last desperate attempt to open the gates of heaven wide, Levi Yitzchak raised his head and cried out to the heavens. "Let them speak, not me," Levi Yitzchak boomed. "Remember the two rubles the widow Sarah paid her son's teacher, instead of spending them on the dress she had longed for. Remember the bowl of soup the Yeshiva student shared with his classmates in spite of the fact that he was starving himself. Remember the bundle of money and the parcel of land Reb Chaim lost because he

—

refused to go back on his word." And so Levi Yitzchak went on and on, listing one by one the simple acts of loving-kindness, unselfishness, and mercy the ordinary men and women of his congregation had performed in the past year. As the congregation raised their eyes, they could see the gates of heaven open completely, and they saw their prayers become a garland and rest on God's head as the Holy One descended from the Seat of Judgment and mounted the Seat of Mercy.

"He formed all their hearts as one heart, and He perceives all their actions as one act," the psalmist insists. When I see this great trembling multitude sitting before me at Neilah, I feel as if I am in the presence of a single trembling heart. All the thousands of gestures — the blowing of a nose, the stifling of a yawn, the wiping away of a tear, a person standing up over there, and one sitting down over there, a child jumping up, another child crying — all these gestures become one single gesture unfolding across the sanctuary in waves and billows. And I look down at the thousands of faces washed over by an innocence so immense that it covers over everyone, and everyone becomes one suffering, innocent heart.

Each face, I now see, has been formed by the same suffering, a suffering that has sunken its cheeks and lined its brow and hooded its eyes. Every face, I now see, is like this; the suffering is visible, like the lines of force on a geological formation, like Levi Yitzchak's supplication and the confession of his congregants, and like the garland of all their prayers taken together, which came to rest on God's head.

And then there comes a point at which I just don't think I can bear to see this anymore, when the weight of the suffering in all these faces just becomes too heartbreaking for me and I feel as

if I have to scream or run away or cry. And just at that moment —
just when I think I can't bear to see this one second more — I see a
great light beneath the suffering in all these faces. I suddenly come
to realize that what I am seeing only looks like suffering, but really
all of it — the sunken skin, the lined brow, the clouded eyes — is
just the convulsions and the lines of force a great love makes as it
struggles to come to the surface of our lives.

And I always feel then that I am standing at the head of an
army of infinite power. I look from face to face. So many of them
have come to share their burdens with me during the year, and I
can see into so many of their hearts. I know that this one has lost a
husband, and this one has lost a son, and this one has lost a father,
and this one envies all of them because she has never had anyone
but has lived alone longing for a family all her life, and this one has
a husband but has never been able to have a child, and this one
has lost his job, and this one has a job but it isn't much of one and
he hates it. He hates to get up in the morning and everyone has
always felt him to be a failure, and this one is a big success but his
wife is leaving him and his children are devastated, and this one
has been devastated by her children who seem to have gone bad
for no reason she can fathom. Certainly it couldn't have been for
lack of love. Nevertheless, they have fallen into a hell-world of
lawlessness and drugs and she can't get them out, and this one has
a child whose mind suddenly stopped working; it isn't an emotional problem; the electrons in her brain just aren't firing properly
anymore, and every day she becomes more confused and her
mother watches helplessly as she sinks into madness, and this one
has been fighting a terrible cancer. It went into remission a few
years ago, but now it is back with a vengeance and she knows she

will die soon. And I look from face to face, and I know that all of these people just go on living day to day as if nothing has happened, quietly, heroically, complaining a little but not nearly as much as they deserve to. They continue to hope, they continue to love, they keep going to work, taking their kids to school, coming to synagogue, and I say to myself, I would go into battle with this army any day of the week.

So every year at Neilah, I declare war on God. I turn the full force of our spiritual armamentarium on God and I say, Give us one more year or else. Give us one more year of life, one more year of sun and rain and wind, one more year to labor and to love on this roiling green-and-blue ball. Give me one more year to love my wife, one more year to watch my children grow. Promise me this or else. Promise me this while there is still a small, charged opening between heaven and earth. Give me one more year of life. Promise me this before the gates come clanging shut.

THE STARS ARE SHINING

ON MY HEAD

SUKKOT

THE STARS ARE SHINING ON THE TOP OF MY HEAD, the wind is in my hair; a few drops of rain are falling into my soup, but the soup is still warm. I am sitting in a sukkah, a booth with branches draped across the top, which I have erected in my backyard. A deep joy is seeping out from the core of my being and filling me body and soul. It began as a kind of lightness. I felt it as soon as the shofar was sounded to signal the end of Yom Kippur. There were three stars in the sky then. I felt all the weight, all the heaviness of the day — all the death and the judgment and the yearning, all the soulful thrashing and beating of breasts — falling away all at once, suddenly gone. I felt light and clean.

The next day I went into my yard with a hammer and started to build my sukkah. Now I am drinking soup in my sukkah, a booth not quite surrounded by walls, with a roof that must admit starlight, and a deep joy is welling up inside me, a curious, naked joy. During the Days of Awe, I was stripped of everything, all my hope, all the illusions to which I had been clinging. Now I feel clean and light and full of joy.

"You shall dwell in booths for seven days," the Torah enjoins us, "so that you will know with every fiber of your being that your ancestors dwelt in booths during their sojourn in the wilderness when they were leaving Egypt." This is a commandment we fulfill not with a gesture or a word, but with our entire body. We sit in the sukkah with our entire body. Only our entire body is capable of knowing what it felt like to leave the burden of Egyptian oppression behind, to let go of it. Egypt in Hebrew is Mitzraim. The root of this word is *tzar*, a narrowness. Egypt was the narrow place. Only the entire body can know what it felt like to be pushed from a place of dire constriction and into a wilderness, a spacious, open world. Only the body can know what it felt like to be born. Only the body can know the fullness of joy, and this is a commandment that can only be fulfilled with joy. All the holidays and all their rituals are to be observed with joy, but there is a special joy, an extra measure of joy, connected to Sukkot. The Torah mentions this requirement three times in connection to Sukkot.

Perhaps this is because Sukkot is the holiday of the fall harvest. While we rejoice at Passover, it is not a full joy, because the spring seedlings are just beginning to come up, just beginning to break the plane of the earth, just beginning to show themselves in the world, and we don't know if they will make it to harvest or not.

We rejoice at Shavuot, but it is only the early harvest, the time of the first fruits, and although there is a special joy in this, there is also anxiety. The full harvest won't be until fall, until Sukkot. But at Sukkot, there is no anxiety. There is nothing to hold back. There is only rejoicing. The full harvest has come.

Or perhaps this special joy we feel at Sukkot is a cathartic joy, a joy in direct proportion to the anxiety of the High Holidays. The high priest has gone into the Holy of Holies, emerged alive, and pronounced the unpronounceable name of God. We will live another year. The rains will come. The crops will grow. We will live.

Or perhaps this special joy is precisely the joy of being stripped naked, the joy of being flush with life, the joy of having nothing between our skin and the wind and the starlight, nothing between us and the world. We have spent the past many weeks stripping ourselves naked — acknowledging our brokenness, allowing ourselves to see what we won't usually look at, embracing the emptiness at the core of our experience, reducing our lives to a series of impulses that rise up and then fall away again. And we have even let the reins of denial slip a little; we have relaxed our fierce determination to ward off death at any cost. We have invited ourselves to entertain the possibility that we might die. On Rosh Hashanah it is written, we acknowledge, who will live and who will die, and by Yom Kippur we have acknowledged that it may very well be us who dies.

So now we sit flush with the world, in a "house" that calls attention to the fact that it gives us no shelter. It is not really a house. It is the interrupted idea of a house, a parody of a house. According to Jewish law, this booth we must dwell in for seven days need only have closed walls on two and a half sides, and we must be able to see the stars through the organic material — the leaves and branches — that constitutes its roof. This is not a house; it is the bare outline of a house. It is like that architectural feature called the broken pediment, the notch in the roofline of the façade of a house which leaves the mind to complete the line, and thus implants the idea of a line in the mind even more forcefully than an unbroken line would. So it is that the sukkah, with its broken lines, its open roof, its walls that don't quite surround us, calls the idea of the house to mind more forcefully than a house itself might do.

And it exposes the idea of a house as an illusion. The idea of a house is that it gives us security, shelter, haven from the storm. But no house can really offer us this. No building of wood and stone can ever afford us protection from the disorder that is always lurking all around us. No shell we put between us and the world can ever really keep us secure from it. And we know this. We never really believed in this illusion. That's why we never felt truly secure in it. The rabbis of the Talmud told a parable:

It is the usual way of human beings to feel secure and unafraid while under the shelter of their own roofs. On emerging from their homes, their sense of security is diminished and they begin to feel fear. Israel, however, is different. While in their homes the whole year, they are apprehensive. But when Sukkot comes and they leave their homes and come under the shadow of the sukkah, their hearts are full of trust, faith, and joy, for now they are protected, not by the protection of their roofs, but by the shadow of their faith and trust in God.

—

The matter may be compared to a person who locks himself up at home for fear of robbers. Regardless of how many locks he uses and how strong these locks may be, he remains afraid lest the locks be broken. Once he hears the voice of the King approaching and calling, "Emerge from your chamber and join me," he is no longer afraid. He immediately opens his doors and emerges joyously to join the King, for wherever the King is, no harm can come to him. He then goes wherever the King leads him, and trust and joy never depart from him.

In the sukkah, a house that is open to the world, a house that freely acknowledges that it cannot be the basis of our security, we let go of this need. The illusion of protection falls away, and suddenly we are flush with our life, feeling our life, following our life, doing its dance, one step after another.

And when we speak of joy here, we are not speaking of fun. Joy is a deep release of the soul, and it includes death and pain. Joy is any feeling fully felt, any experience we give our whole being to. We are conditioned to choose pleasure and to reject pain, but the truth is, any moment of our life fully inhabited, any feeling fully felt, any immersion in the full depth of life, can be the source of deep joy. Such is the testimony of Heschel, one of the elderly Jews of Venice, California, whose wisdom is collected in Barbara Myerhoff's *Number Our Days.*

So I'll tell you how I survive, but you won't like it. Every time I say anything about it, people shudder. But you couldn't get away from it, the thing I am talking about. The word is "pain." Pain is the avenue to getting a soul, getting quality from yourself. Now if you would like to hear a little more, I could give you an example. When I start to talk about pain, it leaves me. That's why I don't like to talk so much. All that I got to say is painful, and when I tell somebody about it, then I feel better. But that's no good. It comes back to you when you're not looking, whoosh, it jumps out from behind the stove and grabs you. So when the pain comes, I am patient. I shut up, active silence. I bear it, wait, even overnight, but I mean I bear it, I don't take a tranquilizer, a sleeping pill, some schnapps, or watch television. I stand before it, I call the pain out. After you go through this, you discover you got choices. You become whole. This is the task of our life. I want to live this kind of life so I can be alive every minute. I want to know when I'm awake, I'm altogether awake. When I'm asleep, I'm asleep.

But few of us could bear to be this awake to our lives. As laudable as this relationship to our experience may be, we will likely find the experience of being flush with reality every single second of our lives to be unbearable, untenable, and otherwise impossible.

In Dashiell Hammett's *The Maltese Falcon*, Sam Spade tells the story of his first case as a private detective. He was called in by a woman to trace the whereabouts of her husband, who had suddenly gone missing. This man had been one of Seattle's leading insurance salesmen. He and his wife had lived in a beautiful house and were well respected in the Seattle community. Then one day, he disappeared without a trace.

Sam Spade tracked this man doggedly for years. Finally he found him in Tacoma, a half-hour's drive from Seattle. Now he was one of Tacoma's leading real estate salesmen. He was married again, and he and his new wife lived in a beautiful house and were pillars of Tacoma society.

Spade was mystified. This man seemed to have stepped out of one life and then replicated it precisely less than half an hour's drive away. Why had he done it? One day at lunchtime, the man explained, he had been walking back to his office in downtown Seattle when a brick fell out of the window of a tall building and came so close to him that it actually grazed his face. This man was thunderstruck. He had very carefully constructed a life that in no way took account of the possibility of a brick falling from a window and killing him. So he left that life straightaway. He hitchhiked to the coast, caught a tramp steamer bound for the South Pacific, and sailed around the world several times. He had adventures in all the great cities of the world. Then little by little, without even realizing what he was doing, he drifted back to the States, settled in Tacoma, became enormously successful again, married another lovely wife, and built another beautiful house.

Sam Spade gave this story the following moral: "He adjusted his life to take into account that bricks fell out of windows, but then bricks stopped falling out of windows." In other words, we cannot bear too much reality.

Form, the Buddhists remind us, is emptiness. Yesh (Being-ness), the Jewish mystics insist, is Aiyin (Nothingness). But emptiness is also form. Aiyin is also Yesh. The forms from which we derive comfort and security may well be an illusion, and may well be a shell that stands between us and our experience. But they are an inescapable illusion, an inevitable shell. Form is an inevitable part of our spiritual landscape. We can't live apart from it.

But once a year, after several months of reconnecting with the emptiness at the core of form, we leave the formal world behind. We sit in a house that is only the idea of a house, a house that calls attention to the illusory nature of all houses.

And there is a joy in this, a joy born of the realization that nothing can protect us. Nothing can save us from death, so it's no use defending ourselves. We may as well give up, and there is a wonderful release in this giving up.

I feel this joy as I sit in the sukkah drinking soup cooled by the rain. Tomorrow morning I will wave the *lulav* and the *etrog*, the four species we are commanded to take up during Sukkot. In my right hand I will hold the long spine of a palm branch, with two willow sprigs tied to its left and three sprigs of myrtle to its right. And in my left hand I will hold a yellow citron full of pocks and ridges, and I will wave these things twice, once as I sing hymns of joy and praise to God, and once as I march around the synagogue in solemn procession crying, "Save me, please! Save me, please!" The sexual imagery couldn't be clearer — the palm frond phallus with the myrtle and willow testes; the ridged and speckled yellow fruit — nor could it be more appropriate. What sex and agriculture have in common is that they point simultaneously to both the power and the impotence of the human condition. We have no idea how to form a human life. We can't make it happen by ourselves, yet we are absolutely indispensable to the process. We have no idea how a seed bears fruit. We can't make that happen either. Yet if we don't plant the seed and nurture it and water it and harvest it, no fruit will ever come. These things can't happen without us, but neither can we make them happen on our own.

So tomorrow morning I will walk around the synagogue celebrating both our power and our impotence, our miraculous capacity to bear and nurture life, and our utter dependence on God for it, and I will feel a deep sense of joy as I do, because this is the truth of my life. This is the cusp I actually stand on at every moment of my life. Every moment of my life, I am utterly powerless and infinitely powerful. Every moment of my life, I am inescapably hammered into place by everything that has ever happened since the creation of the universe, and every moment I am free to act in a way that will alter the course of that great flow of being forever.

And here at the core of our life, here at its paradoxical center, there is a mysterious, inexplicable, senseless joy.

The poet Gerald Stern captures this joy quite precisely in the poem "Lucky Life."

Dear waves, what will you do for me this year?
Will you drown out my scream?
Will you let me rise through the fog?
Will you fill me with that old salt feeling?
Will you let me take my long steps in the cold sand?
Will you let me lie on the white bedspread and study
the black clouds with the blue holes in them?
Will you let me see the rusty trees and the old monoplanes
one more year?
Will you still let me draw my sacred figures
and move the kites and the birds around with my dark
mind?

—

Lucky life is like this. Lucky there is an ocean to come to.
Lucky you can judge yourself in this water.
Lucky you can be purified over and over again.
Lucky there is the same cleanliness for everyone.
Lucky life is like that. Lucky life. Oh lucky life.
Oh lucky lucky life. Lucky life.

This is the overwhelming, senseless gratitude we feel when we are finally fully awake. And it makes no difference what we awaken to, whether it is to pain or to pleasure, to life or to death; it is all of a piece, all the ground of a deep joy when fully inhabited, when wholly attended to.

Nor does it make any difference that we will inevitably sleep again, that we will drift back into our house or one remarkably like it without even realizing that we have. It makes no difference that there will once again be walls between us and the rest of the world.

In the fullness of time, these walls will also fall down, and a great horn will sound, calling us to wakefulness again.

☒ ☒ ☒ Acknowledgments ☒ ☒ ☒

This book would not have been written if my agent, Arielle Eckstut, of James Levine Communications, Inc., had not come to my office one day and demanded that I write it. Her encouragement, support, wit, and taste have become an important part of my work as a writer.

Deborah Baker, my editor at Little, Brown and Company, made this book immeasurably better. She is a tough and loving editor, and the one quality was as important to me as the other in writing this book. The care and time she devoted to this project, her belief in it, her incredible editing skill, and her friendship were all invaluable.

My wife, Sherril Jaffe, herself a brilliant writer and teacher of writing, is the best first reader any writer could possibly have.

—

I am indebted to a number of rabbinic colleagues for their ideas, inspiration, and source material. It was in the masterly sermons of Rabbi Jack Riemer that I first saw the ruminations on the Avaryonim (Chapter 8), the Shlomo Carlebach story about forgiveness (Chapter 9), and the Rudolph Giuliani story (also Chapter 9). I first read the story about the rabbi, the cantor, and the videotape (Chapter 6) in a Rosh Hashanah sermon by Rabbi Mitchell Wohlberg. Among the myriad sources I quoted in my discussion of spiritual renewal (Chapter 7), some were from a sermon by Rabbi Dov Peretz Elkins, and others were from Yitzhak Buxbaum's compilation, *Jewish Spiritual Practices.*

Close readers of this book may notice that I sometimes offer different versions of the same biblical and liturgical passages in different locations. The vast majority of these translations are my own. Translation is always an interpretation, a process of selection from a range of possible and equally authentic meanings. Rather than offering the same translations of these texts in every case, I chose to stress those shades of suggested meaning that best illuminated the point under discussion in each particular context. Translations of the High Holiday liturgy that were not my own were taken from *The Rabbinical Assembly Mahzor for Rosh Hashanah and Yom Kippur,* Rabbi Jules Harlow, editor.

Finally, I would like to thank the members of my synagogue, Congregation Beth Sholom of San Francisco, for honoring me by opening their hearts and their lives to me. This book is my love song to them.

COPYRIGHT ACKNOWLEDGMENTS

—

ABOUT THE AUTHOR

Rabbi Alan Lew has been the spiritual leader of Congregation Beth Sholom in San Francisco since 1991. Rabbi Lew is the founder and director of Makor Or, the first meditation center connected to a synagogue. He is the author of numerous works of poetry and *One God Clapping: The Spiritual Path of a Zen Rabbi*, which won the PEN Josephine Miles Award for Literary Excellence. Prior to his ordination as a rabbi in 1988 at the Jewish Theological Seminary in New York, he received a B.A. from the University of Pennsylvania and an M.F.A. from the University of Iowa Writers' Workshop. Rabbi Lew is married to the novelist Sherril Jaffe.

CPSIA information can be obtained at www.ICGtesting.com
Printed in the USA
LVOW06*0250170915

454471LV00001B/1/P